User Manual for the Data-Series Interface of the Gr Application Software

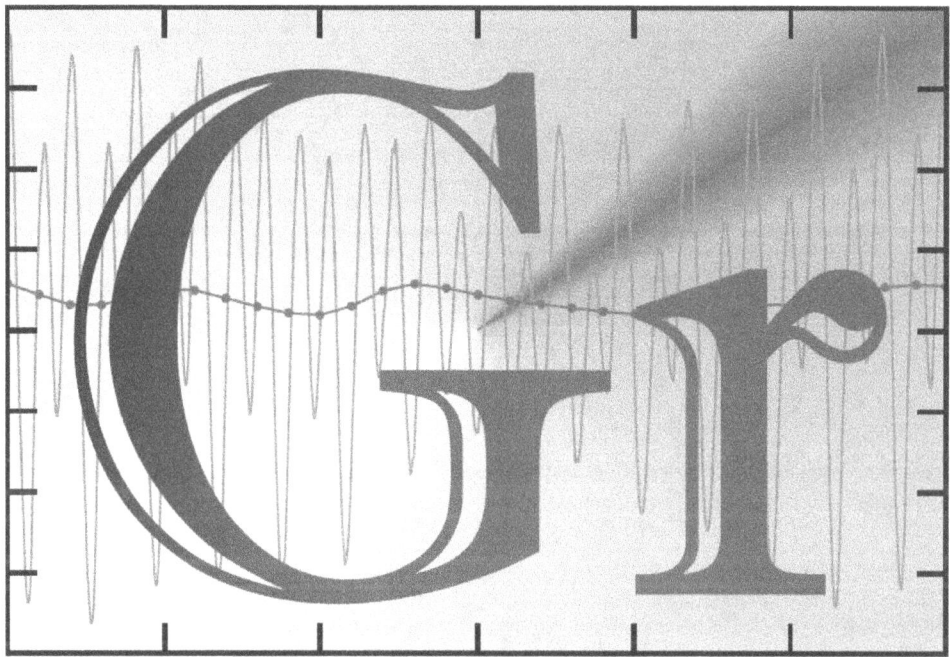

Open-File Report 2009–1181

U.S. Department of the Interior
U.S. Geological Survey

User Manual for the Data-Series Interface of the Gr Application Software

By John M. Donovan

Open-File Report 2009–1181

U.S. Department of the Interior
U.S. Geological Survey

U.S. Department of the Interior
KEN SALAZAR, Secretary

U.S. Geological Survey
Marcia K. McNutt, Director

U.S. Geological Survey, Reston, Virginia: 2009

For more information on the USGS—the Federal source for science about the Earth, its natural and living resources, natural hazards, and the environment, visit http://www.usgs.gov or call 1-888-ASK-USGS
For an overview of USGS information products, including maps, imagery, and publications,
visit http://www.usgs.gov/pubprod

To order this and other USGS information products, visit http://store.usgs.gov

Any use of trade, product, or firm names is for descriptive purposes only and does not imply endorsement by the

U.S. Government.

Suggested citation:
Donovan, J.M., 2010, User manual for the data-series interface of Gr application software: U.S. Geological Survey Open-File Report, 43 p.

Contents

Abstract 1

Introduction..1

    Download and Installation 1

    System Requirements 1

    Installing and Running on Windows 2

Working in Gr...2

    Using Multiple Pages 2

    Opening a File 3

    Displaying Data 4

Graph and Page Layout..4

    Changing the Graph and Page Layout..5

The Properties Dialog...6

    Dialog Layout 6

    The Gr Object Tree..7

    The Properties Table 8

    Common Object Properties 8

Modes 14

Zooming and Panning 15

    Zooming with the Mouse 15

    Zoom Commands...16

The Status Bar...16

    The Default Status Bar..16

    The Detailed Status Bar..17

Selecting and Dragging Data Points 19

    Selecting Points 19

    Deleting Points 20

    Dragging Points 20

The Modify Dialog..20

    Choosing an Operation 21

    Interpolation..22

    Output 22

Cutting, Copying, and Pasting Curves 24

Undoing Operations...24

Tools 25

    Fillers and Filters...25

    Drawing New Curves..26

Page Formats..27

Saving As XML 27

Saving as GS Format 27

Printing...28

Templates 31

Summary...31
References Cited..31
Appendix A.   File Format Descriptions..32
    Gr XML Format..32
    GS Format...33
    Reading the Header..33
    Reading the Body...34
    Writing GS Format..34
Other Data Formats...34
Appendix B.   Scripting...37
Appendix C.   Tips for Working with Red-Green-Blue (RGB) Colors...39
Appendix D.   Symbol Indexes...42
Appendix E.   Contact Information..43

Figures

Figure 1.   The Gr Application Icon   2

Figure 2.   Opening screen of the Gr Application   3

Figure 3.   The File Options Dialog Window in the Gr Application   4

Figure 4.   The order in which specific colors and patterns are assigned to curves that are
added to a graph in the Gr Application   5

Figure 5.   Example of repositioning a graph (speed in feet per second) within a window
in the Gr Application   6

Figure 6.   The Properties Dialog window in the Gr Application   7

Figure 7.   The Gr Application showing certain graph properties and the accompanying
graphs   11

Figure 8.   The Gr Application, showing certain axis properties and the accompanying
graphs.   13

Figure 9.   Example of properties for each graph shown in the Properties Dialog box,
and curves that have been modified within the top graph in the Gr Application ...   15

Figure 10.   Example of the Mode Panel box that uses radio buttons to indicate the current
mode in the Gr Application   15

Figure 11.   An example of an area selected for zooming within a graph in the
Gr Application   16

Figure 12.   The Default Status Bar, as shown in the Gr Application   16

Figure 13.   Available format descriptors (left column) and their respective outputs
(right column), as shown in the Gr Application   17

Figure 14.   The Detailed Status Bar, as shown in the Gr Application   17

Figure 15.   Panel 1 of the Detailed Status Bar, as shown in the Gr Application   18

Figure 16.   Panel 2 of the Detailed Status Bar, as shown in the Gr Application   18

Figure 17.   Panel 3 of the Detailed Status Bar, as shown in the Gr Application   19

Figure 18.   Panel 4 of the Detailed Status Bar, as shown in the Gr Application   19

Figure 19.   An example of a Selected Point in a graph, as shown in the Gr Application   20

Figure 20.   The Modify Dialog window, as shown in the Gr Application   21

Figure 21. An example of two parabolas (solid lines) fitted through four points and averaged to find the solution (dashed line) that is used with parabolic interpolation in the Gr Application 22

Figure 22. An example of resampling from a longer interval to a shorter interval using parabolic interpolation as shown in the Gr Application 23

Figure 23. Resampling from an interval of two (solid line) to an interval of nine using linear interpolation (dashed line) and linear averaging (dotted line), as shown in the Gr Application 24

Figure 24. Gap filling techniques for graphs in the Gr Application 25

Figure 25. Applying the Godin filter to a selected curve in a graph in the Gr Application 26

Figure 26. The result of applying the Godin filter in a graph in the Gr Application 26

Figure 27. The scale at which the graph was printed and at which the Line Point Reduction command is performed in the Gr Application 29

Figure 28. Detail showing the points that were used to define the line with a Line Point Reduction width scale of 0.25, as shown in the Gr Application 29

Figure 29. Detail showing the points that were used to define the line with a Line Point Reduction width scale of 2.0, as shown in the Gr Application 29

Figure 30. Detail showing the points that were used to define the line with a Line Point Reduction width scale of 10.0, as shown in the Gr Application 30

Figure 31. PostScript output of a black curve with a Line Point Reduction width scale of 10 over a red curve with Line Point Reduction width scale of 0, as shown in the Gr Application 30

Tables

1. The color and pattern of each line added to a graph 4

Appendix tables:

C1. Examples of basic Red-Green-Blue (RGB) color system combinations 40

C2. Examples of ranges of Red-Green-Blue (RGB) color system values 41

D1. The available symbols, associated indexes, and appearance on postscript output 42

This page intentionally left blank.

User Manual for the Data-Series Interface of the Gr Application Software

By John M. Donovan

Abstract

This manual describes the data-series interface for the Gr Application software. Basic tasks such as plotting, editing, manipulating, and printing data series are presented. The properties of the various types of data objects and graphical objects used within the application, and the relationships between them also are presented. Descriptions of compatible data-series file formats are provided.

Introduction

Gr is a visualization and analysis application for displaying, editing, and printing X-Y data. It can be used to display or animate vector data, particle paths, or two-dimensional (2D) data fields, but only the data-series interface is described in this document. Gr works with any data series that describes Y as a function of X, that is an ordered set of X-Y pairs. These pairs could represent points in space or form a time series, which is an ordered set of time-value pairs. Gr allows the user to zoom in and out and pan within a graph. It also offers several ways to edit or manipulate data, and can accept data in several file formats.

Gr was developed for use by members of the U.S. Geological Survey (USGS) San Francisco Bay Hydrodynamics Project in Sacramento, California. The Gr source code is freely available (Free Software Foundation, accessed March 24, 2008) and was written using the Java platform (Sun Microsystems, accessed March 24, 2008), OpenGL (OpenGL.org, accessed March 24, 2008), and JOGL (JOGL, accessed March 24, 2008). The program runs on Windows primarily, but it can be ported to other platforms.

Download and Installation

To use the latest version of Gr, the user first must download the program from the Gr web site at *http://ca.water.usgs.gov/ program/sfbay/gr/*. Under the Downloads heading, locate the desired type of platform and download the required distribution files. The Gr web site contains links to one or more files for each supported platform. If a platform contains more than one file, the first file is a base installation that includes everything required to run Gr and the other files contain updates to portions of the base installation.

System Requirements

To run Gr, Java 6 [Java Runtime Environment (JRE) 6] must be installed. See the link to the JRE on the Gr web site for installation. The minimum recommended configuration for Windows is a Pentium III with 256 MB of memory and a graphics card that performs geometry acceleration. The computer should be running in 16-bit color mode, or higher, at a resolution of at least 800X600. Gr should function properly on all versions of Windows.

The current version of Gr is available only for the 32-bit Windows platform (Microsoft, accessed March 24, 2008). Older versions of Gr are available for Solaris for SPARC, SGI Irix, and Linux for x86 (Linux Online, accessed March 24, 2008). To obtain the latest version of Gr for these platforms, or for Mac OS X or other 64-bit operating systems, contact the author of this report.

Installing and Running on Windows

When JRE 1.5 is downloaded from the Gr web site and installed on a Windows system, it creates a directory within C:\Program Files\Java. Unzip the gr_win_XXX.zip distribution to the *C:* directory, and a C:\Program Files\USGS\Gr directory will be created that includes the Gr libraries and gr.bat file documentation. If Gr or Java are installed in locations other than the defaults, the gr.bat file must be edited to use the correct paths.

If the user is upgrading or installing Gr in a different directory, or the gr.bat file had to be modified, a copy of gr.bat must be made before the file is overwritten with a new version of Gr. The paths in the batch file will need to be changed from their default values.

To run Gr, double click gr.bat or drag a file and drop it on gr.bat. Alternately, gr.bat filename can be typed in a command window, where "filename" is the name of a file Gr recognizes. After Gr is running, a file can be opened by dragging and dropping it anywhere within the Gr window.

In addition to the Gr application itself, a console window will appear in which Java writes text errors or status messages output. It is recommended that a shortcut be created on the desktop to C:\Program Files\USGS\Gr\gr.bat. This can be done by dragging the batch file from the Gr directory and dropping it on the desktop while holding down the Ctrl and Shift keys. There is a Gr icon image in the C:\Program Files\USGS\Gr directory called gr64X256.ico that can be used with the shortcut or Gr data files. To use it with the batch file, right-click on the shortcut and choose *Properties*. On the *Shortcut* tab, click *Change Icon...* navigate to the *C:\Program Files\USGS\Gr directory* and select the gr64X256.ico file (*fig. 1*).

Figure 1.   The Gr Application Icon.

Working in Gr

Gr shows multiple graphs in the format that would appear on a printed page (*fig. 2*). It is not exactly "what you see is what you get," but it is close. The page area has a default color of black and takes up most of the frame on the Gr main window. Several menus are listed across the top and a column of buttons is displayed down the left side of the window. Clicking any of the buttons is the same as choosing a command from the menu or using the keyboard shortcut. Status information, such as the current operating mode, is given at the bottom of the window.

Using Multiple Pages

Gr can have any number of pages open, but it only displays one at a time. To create a new page, click the *New* button under the *Page* heading on the toolbar, or choose *New Page* from the *Page* menu. To advance to the next page once multiple pages are open, click the *Next* button under the *Page* heading. To delete the current page, click the *Delete* button under the *Page* heading and then click *OK* on the confirmation dialog window that appears.

Usually, any operation performed in Gr affects only the current page. The exception to this "rule" happens when an operation that was previously applied to a different page is undone. Since the same object can appear on multiple pages, changing the object on one page will cause it to change on all pages that it appears.

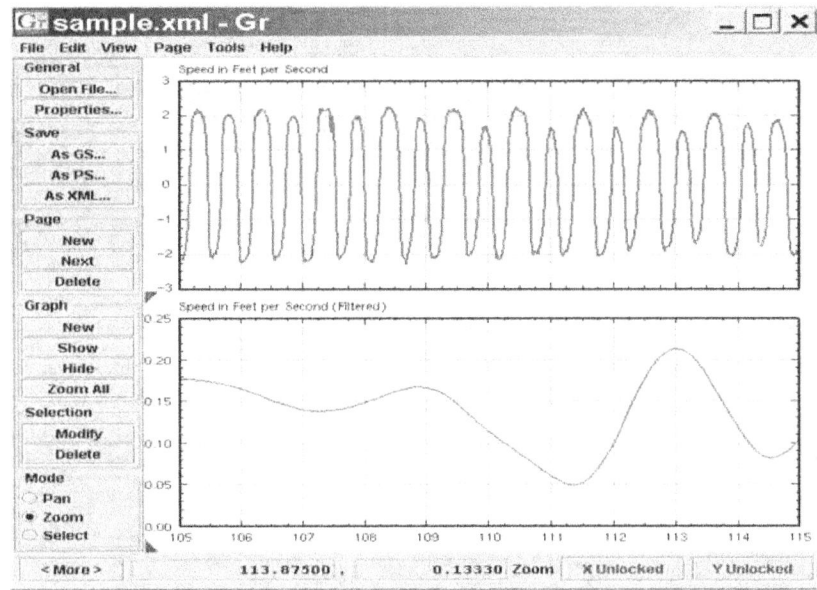

Figure 2. Opening screen of the Gr Application.

Opening a File

The data displayed by Gr typically is loaded from a formatted file that usually consists of columns of data with an optional heading across the top of the frame. Several different formats are recognized and the most common format specifications are detailed in *Appendix A*. Gr recognizes some formats from the file name extension and others from analyzing the first few lines of that file. The user may be asked to specify or confirm which format is being used.

To open a file, click the *Open File...* button, or select it from the *File* menu (Ctrl+Shift+O). A dialog box will appear showing the directory of the last file opened or, if none has been opened, the user's home directory.

Using the *Open File* dialog, navigate to the directory containing the data file to be opened, and double-click on it. Once a file is chosen, Gr usually will display the *File Options* dialog box to confirm the type of file that is being opened and to give the option of either overlaying it on the current page or opening it on a new page (*fig. 3*). For some file formats, additional options are available by clicking the *Options...* button. If no options are available for the selected file type, the *Options...* button will be disabled.

If a file ends in a known extension, the *File Options* dialog will not be displayed. The recognized extensions are .xml for XML project files, .gs for GS data files, and .grs for Gr script files. These files are opened without showing the confirmation dialog and are overlaid on the current page. If an XML project file is opened, and it defines its own page, then a new page will be created. If Gr does not recognize the file extension, it will read the first few lines of the file and attempt to determine the file type.

Before Gr opens a file, it checks for a script file called gr_config.grs in the same directory and executes it if it is present. Typically, the configuration file is used to set the default data format with a line similar to the following.

```
SetFormat "gov.usgs.sfhydro.data.CR10DataFile"
```

After reading the configuration file, Gr opens the data file, if it can be opened, and its data will be displayed in one or more graphs on the page. If there is a problem opening the file, an error dialog window will appear or error messages will be written to the Java console window.

Multiple files can be opened at once by holding down the Ctrl key and selecting the files in the *Open File* dialog. This command causes each of the files to be opened individually.

A complete description of Gr compatible file formats is available in *Appendix A*.

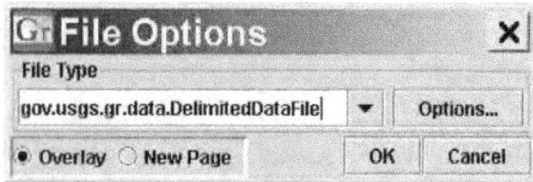

Figure 3.   The File Options Dialog Window in the Gr Application.

Displaying Data

When a file is opened, one or more graphs are stacked vertically on the screen. Each graph has its own Y-Axis, but shares a common X-Axis. Only the bottom graph is allowed to display labels or a title on its X-Axis. Gr displays a single column of graphs, but the default setting can be modified after opening data.

Some file formats, such as GS, assign a numerical data type to each data series in the file. Gr attempts to group curves of the same data types on the same graph, regardless of which graphs are selected or hidden. If a new data type is encountered, a new graph will be created and added to the page. Gr determines the data type for a graph by identifying the data type of the first curve within a graph. If the new data are not visible after overlaying, use the *Show Graph* command or invoke the *Zoom All* command. Take care to ensure that the new curve is not being drawn over an existing curve.

When multiple curves are added to a graph, each uses a different color and line pattern (*table 1*; *fig. 4*).

Graph and Page Layout

Each graph consists of a rectangular frame containing one or more curves representing data, and optional labels, tick marks, and grid lines. The graphs are stretched to fit the page and are numbered from the bottom of the page upward, starting with number one. Hiding or showing a graph does not change its index number as does deleting or moving it. There is no set limit to the number of graphs that can be displayed on a page, but they become progressively smaller and harder to distinguish as the number of graphs increases. Hiding some of the graphs on a page will make the displayed graphs larger and easier to see. Or, some of the graphs can be placed on another page using the *New Page* command.

Table 1.   The color and pattern of each line added to a graph.

Line number	Color	Line pattern
1	Green	Solid
2	Magenta	Dashed
3	Cyan	Dotted
4	Yellow	Dash-dot
5	White	Loose dash
6	Red Green	Loose dotted
7	Green	Dash-dot-dash
8	Green	Tight dashed
9	Green	Tight dotted
10	Green	Solid

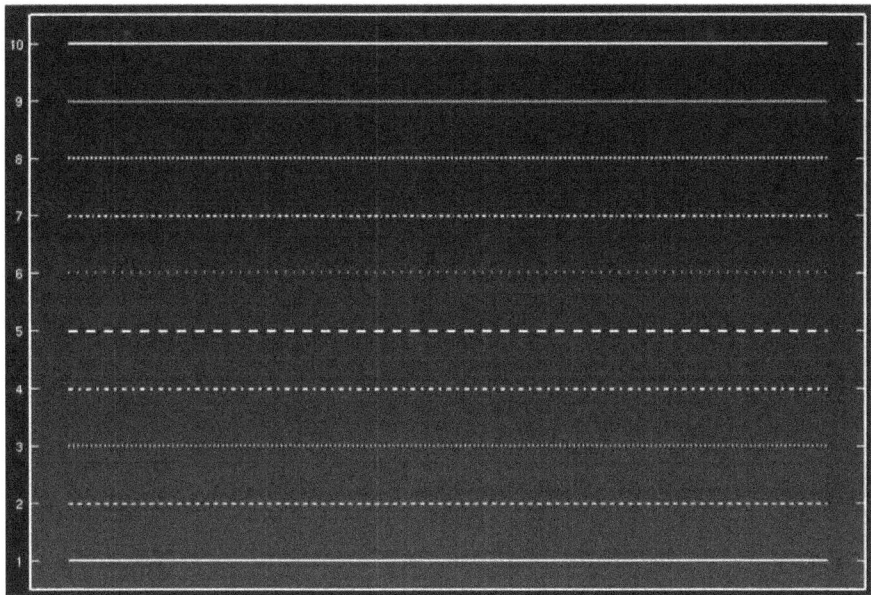

Figure 4. The order in which specific colors and patterns are assigned to curves that are added to a graph in the Gr Application.

At any given time, one or more graphs may be selected for action. Selected graphs are indicated with dark green markers at the left corners of their areas of the page. To select a graph, move the mouse cursor over it and click any mouse button. This also will deselect all other graphs. To add a graph to the current selection, hold the Ctrl key down and select the additional graph with the mouse. Holding down the Alt key will deselect the graph beneath the mouse cursor, and select all others. Holding down Ctrl and Alt together works the same as holding down Alt, however, previously deselected graphs will remain deselected. When editing points in *Select* mode, only one graph can be selected at a time.

Changing the Graph and Page Layout

A graph can be hidden or deleted once it is selected. To hide a graph, select it and press the *Hide* button under the *Graph* heading on the tool bar, or select *Hide Graph* from the *Page* menu (Ctrl+H). A graph can be deleted by any of three ways: (1) press the *Delete* key on the keyboard or (2) click the *Delete* button under the *Selection* heading on the tool bar, or (3) choose *Delete* from the *Edit* menu. A dialog box asking for confirmation of the action will appear. If points or curves are selected within a graph, the Delete key will delete only those selected and not the graph itself.

To show a graph that has been hidden, press the *Show* button under the *Graph* heading on the tool bar, or select the command from the *Page* menu (Alt+S). The hidden graph with the lowest index will be restored to the spot on the page indicated by its number. For example, if graphs 1 and 3 are showing and graph 2 is hidden, graph 2 will be restored to its place above graph 1 and below graph 3.

To move a graph to a different location on the page, move the mouse cursor to within a few pixels of the left edge of the graph's area, and wait for a gray bar to appear. When the bar appears, press and hold either the left or right mouse button, and drag the graph to the desired location. As the graph moves, other graphs will move to make room for it (*fig. 5*). When the mouse button is released, the graph will snap into the empty slot. Dragging the mouse cursor out of the page drawing area also will cause the selected graph to snap into the empty slot.

New, empty graphs can be created by clicking *New* under the *Graph* heading on the toolbar, or selecting *New Graph* (Ctrl+N) from the *Page* menu. An empty graph will be created and added to the top of the page and given the next available index number. See the sections on overlaying data files, pasting curves, and the draw command for ways to add data to the empty graph.

The Properties Dialog

Nearly every object displayed in Gr can be controlled using the *Edit Properties* dialog box (Properties Dialog) (*fig. 6*). To open the dialog, click the *Properties...* button on the toolbar, or select it from the *Page* menu (Ctrl+Shift+R). The initial size of the dialog is proportional to the computer screen size, but the dialog can be resized after it is open by dragging the sides or corners with the mouse. The dialog box is "modal," meaning that the main Gr window will not respond to input until the dialog is closed.

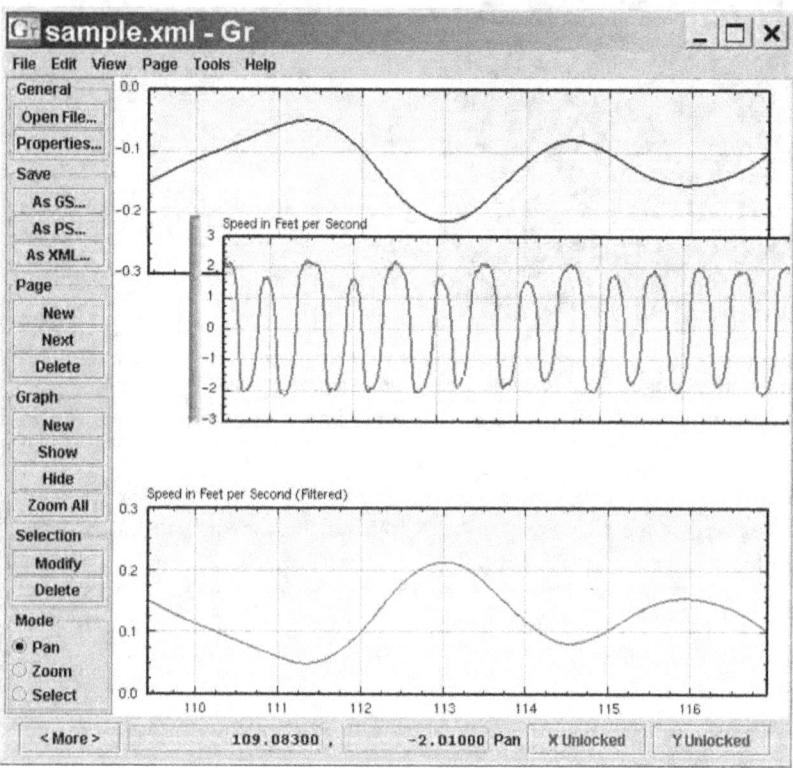

Figure 5.   Example of repositioning a graph (speed in feet per second) within a window in the Gr Application.

Dialog Layout

The Properties Dialog is divided into two areas: a top pane, containing the Gr object tree, and a bottom pane, containing a properties table. Scroll bars automatically appear around the edges of these areas if they hold more information than can be displayed at once. A splitter bar separates the two areas and can be dragged with the mouse to adjust the amount of space given to each area.

There are three buttons at the bottom of the dialog box for closing and applying changes. The *OK* button applies all the changes in the dialog box to the affected objects and then closes the dialog. The *Apply* button applies all the values for viewing in the main Gr window but leaves the dialog box open for other modifications. The *Cancel* button closes the dialog without applying the selected changes.

The Gr Object Tree

The upper pane of the Properties Dialog contains an expandable tree representing every object within Gr. Every object has a "parent" that is higher in the tree, and some objects have "children" that are lower in the tree. The hierarchy displayed in the tree pane depicts the objects as they are stored by Gr and the way they would be saved in an XML file.

The exact appearance of the tree is dependent on the current Java Look and Feel (LAF); however, no matter which LAF is used, there are always similarities in the way the tree is drawn. Each node is drawn on a line by itself that contains an icon, a short, generic description, and an optional title. If the node has children, a marker is drawn to the left of the icon, which indicates whether the children currently are being shown. To expand a node (so the children are showing), click once on the marker. To collapse it (so that the children are hidden), click the marker again and it will toggle back to the original state.

To select a tree node, you can click anywhere on the icon or name. This also deselects any previously selected nodes. To select multiple nodes at once, hold down the Ctrl button and click on each additional node. To select a continuous range of nodes, click the first node, hold down the Shift key, then click on the last node.

Once one or more nodes have been selected, a right-click on the mouse will display a context-sensitive menu. If no nodes are selected, the only available menu command is *Apply All Changes*, which is identical to clicking the *Apply* button at the bottom of the dialog. If one or more nodes are selected, the menu will contain the additional items: *Cut* and *Copy*.

Choosing *Cut* from the right mouse menu removes the selected nodes from the tree and stores them in the Properties Dialog's clipboard, thereby overwriting the contents. The *Copy* menu item does the same thing without removing the selected nodes. Once nodes have been added to the clipboard, they can be added as children to any other node. To do this, click on the target parent node or nodes, then right click. This menu will have two additional items: *Paste Original* and *Paste New Copy*. The *Paste Original* command adds a shared instance of every node in the clipboard to every selected node. This is conceptually the same as pasting a link. The *Paste New Copy* command creates a deep copy (including children) of every node in the clipboard and adds the copies to every selected node. Changing properties or children of a recently copied object affects only that object and leaves the original unchanged.

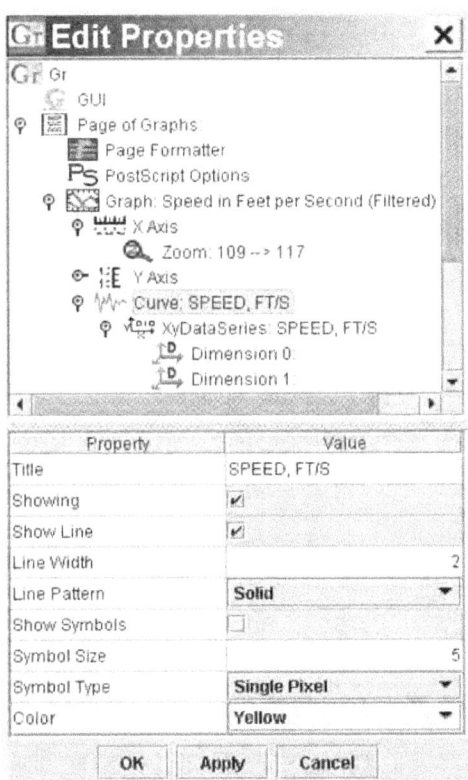

Figure 6.   The Properties Dialog window in the Gr Application.

To add a new object to a selected node, right click and browse through the *Add New* submenu. Several object types are available, such as *Page* and *Graph*.

All the changes to the nodes are stored and applied if the user clicks *Apply* or *OK*, and discarded if the user clicks *Cancel*.

Certain object types will show an additional menu item when selected and right clicked. For instance, file objects show a *Gr File* submenu with items *Save* and *Save As*. Because these commands are applied immediately to the object, they should be used with care and any other changes should be applied first.

Occasionally, the tree in the Properties Dialog will not accurately represent the structure of underlying objects. This usually happens when pasting a second instance of an object when there is room for only one, or when giving a menu command such as *Calculate*. An example of the first case is pasting a *Zoom* object into an *Axis* object. An *Axis* can have only one *Zoom* child, but both will be shown until the Properties Dialog is closed and reopened. An example of the second case is giving the *Calculate* command on a *ParticleAnimationCalculator* object. The calculator adds a new *ParticleAnimation* object to itself, but it isn't visible until the Properties Dialog is closed and reopened. This is a known limitation of the current implementation of Gr.

The Properties Table

The lower pane of the Properties Dialog contains a table with two columns and a variable number of rows. The left column has the heading *Property* and the right column has the heading *Value*. You can adjust the size of the columns by clicking on the dividing line between the headings and dragging to one side or the other.

The properties displayed in the table depend on which nodes are selected in the tree pane above it. Each object has its own set of properties. If more than one node is selected, the table looks through the property lists for properties and displays only those with the same name. For example, if a *Graph* and a *PageOfGraphs* is selected, the only common properties are *Title* and *Show Title*, which would be the only ones displayed in the table. If the current values of the properties vary between the selected objects, the values of the first node selected will be displayed. This allows the properties of multiple objects to be changed simultaneously.

None of the changes made to the properties are applied to the original objects until the *Apply* or *OK* buttons are clicked. Even then, the only properties that are applied are those that have been edited by the user since the last *Apply* event.

For all the text fields, the standard Windows keyboard shortcuts can be used: Ctrl+X to cut, Ctrl+C to copy, and Ctrl+V to paste. Values that exceed the size of the text fields can be inserted, but the arrows on the keyboard must be used to move the cursor and view text within the field.

Common Object Properties

The children of the root Gr object usually consist of one graphical user interface (*GUI*) object, zero or more *Page* objects, and zero or more *File* objects.

The GUI object controls certain options in the Gr Graphical User Interface, and two properties are associated with the object:

GUI Look and Feel	Causes the program to resemble a particular window system such as Microsoft Windows or Motif. The default is Metal, the main LAF for Java on all platforms.
Levels of Undo	The number of operations that are stored that can be undone later.

File objects, such as *XMLProjectFile*, contain links to other objects in the hierarchy. The children are displayed with a generic appearance, and their properties cannot be edited. The properties of the file itself include:

Title	The type of file. This cannot be edited.
File	The name of the disk file to which the data would be saved.

The *Open File...* button brings up a dialog used to choose a file name without saving to the disk. To be safe, changes to the *File* property should be applied before saving the file.

The *PageofGraphs* object contains three properties. The first two properties, *Title* and *Show Title*, are found in nearly every graphical object.

Title	The title of the page
Show Title	Whether to show the title.
Formatter	The Java class that should be used to format the page and the objects on it. The default is *PageFormatter*. Alternatives include *WorkingFormatter* and *ReportFormatter*. Formats can also be applied from the Tools menu.

Pages can have a number of child objects. There always is one formatter and one *PostScript Options* child (Adobe Systems Inc., 1985; 1990). Pages also can contain graphical objects, especially *Graph* objects. Most of the page formatters have no options. The *VariableSizeFormatter* has at least one property.

Number of Values	The number of graphs for which the formatter will make space. Extra graphs are assigned the remaining space. You must close the Properties Dialog and reopen it after you increase this value to see the new Percent (Pct.) properties.
Pct. Size of Graph X	The percentage of the vertical area that should be given to the Xthgraph, where X is the graph index. The *Number of Values* property determines the number of *Pct. Of Graph X* properties shown.

The *PostScript Options* object has several properties that control the page format when saved to a PostScript file. The properties include the following:

File Name	The default file name for saving PostScript output.
Landscape Orientation	Whether to rotate the plot to use landscape orientation.
Font	The name of the PostScript font to use.
Font Size	The size of the PostScript font to use.
Color Curves	Whether to draw each curve with the same color shown on the screen (they are made slightly darker to improve visibility on a white page).
Color Background	Whether to draw the background the same color as it is on the screen.
Line Width	The scale to use for thickening or thinning lines. For curves, the screen line width is multiplied by this number to convert from pixels to points
Uniform Line Width	Whether all lines should be drawn the same width.
Symbol Size	The scale to use for drawing symbols on curves
Reduce Points on Lines	Whether to apply the point reduction algorithm to lines.
Line Reduction Tolerance	The width scale parameter for point reduction of lines.
Reduce Points on Symbols	Whether to apply the point reduction algorithm to symbols.
Symbol Reduction Tolerance	The width scale parameter for point reduction of symbols.
Debug Point Reduction	Whether to show before and after data for point reduction.

See the Printing section in this manual for detailed information about these properties.

Graph objects contain one X Axis, one Y Axis, and any number of graphical objects, especially Curve objects (*fig. 7*). Each graph has the following properties:

Title	The title that is written above the graph.
Show Title	Whether to show the title.
Showing	Whether the graph itself should be shown on the page.
Show X Labels	Whether the X axis labels should be drawn. This is overridden by all the page formatters except VariableSizeFormatter.

To use the Properties Dialog to change the graphs from *figure 7A* to *7B*, the user would expand the tree to show the *Graph* nodes, selecting the first graph and checking the *Showing* check box, then selecting the other two graphs and typing in titles and checking their respective properties.

The *X Axis* and *Y Axis* objects each contain one *Zoom* object, which describes the limits and tick increments of the axis. The axes themselves have the following properties:

Title	The title that should be displayed. A '\n' represents a line break.
Show Title	Whether to show the title next to the axis.
Dimension	The dimension with which this axis is associated (0 for X, 1 for Y). This property is not editable.
Show Major Ticks	Whether to show the major tick marks.
Show Minor Ticks	Whether to show the minor tick marks.
Show Labels	Whether to show numbered labels beside each major tick.
Show Grid	Whether to show grid lines at each major tick mark.

The *Zoom* object controls the area that is displayed in the graph, as well as the tick and label increments used on the axes (*fig. 8*). It has these properties:

View Min	The lower bounds of the current view.
View Max	The upper bounds of the current view.
Outer Min	The lowest value the graph can display by panning.
Outer Max	The highest value the graph can display by panning.
Major Inc	The increment between major tick marks.
Minor Inc	The increment between minor tick marks.
Tick Offset	The starting point from which major ticks are measured.
Unit Scale	The multiplier for units displayed on the axis.
Label Format	A string describing the precision to use for the number labels. For example, "0" indicates no decimal place, "0.00" indicates two decimal places, and "0.0#" indicates at least one place, and at most two, depending on the number.

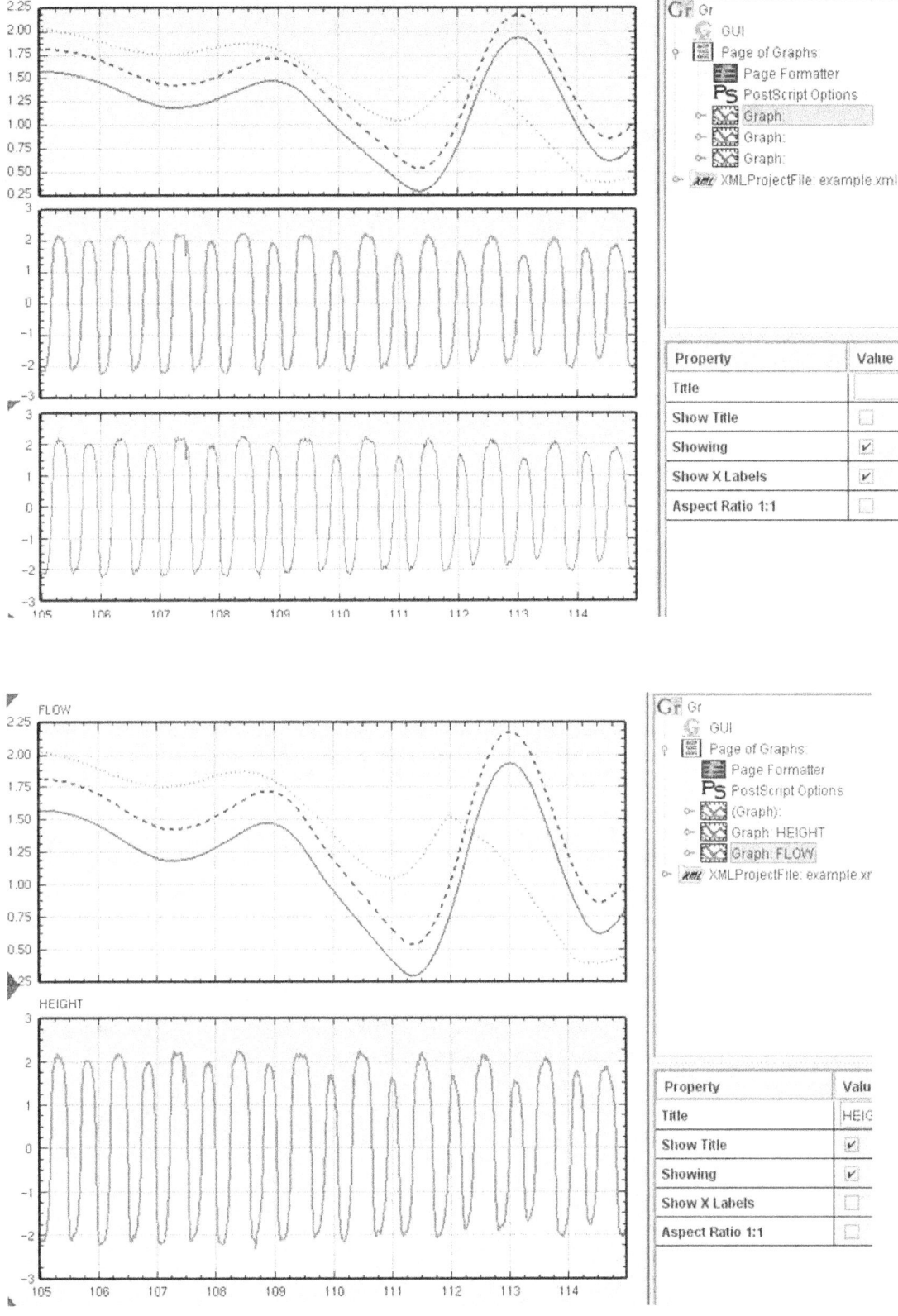

Figure 7.   The Gr Application showing certain graph properties and the accompanying graphs. Changes were made to the properties in (A) to create (B).

Additional format specifications are described in the Java documentation for the class `java.text.DecimalFormat.`, available at *http://java.sun.com/javase/6/docs/api/java/text/DecimalFormat.html*

To use the Properties Dialog to change the graphs from *figure 8A* to *8B*, the user would expand the tree to show the *Graph* nodes, then select the first graph showing, then finally check the box next to *Show X Label*. Then, expand the graphs and their axis nodes. Select the Y axis of the first graph showing and uncheck the *Show Minor Ticks* check box, then select the other *Zoom* node within it and set *View Min* to "-10", *View Max* to "10" and *Major Inc* to "5". To use the Properties Dialog to change the graphs from (*B*) to (*C*), the user would select the *Zoom* node within the last graph's *Y axis* node and set *View Min* to "0.2", *View Max* to "5", *Major Inc* to "2", *Minor Inc* to "0.5", and *Offset* to "1".

The *Curve* object controls how a two-dimensional data series is drawn within a graph. Each contains one data-series object, which stores the X–Y data (*fig. 9*).

Title	The title of the curve. This is shared with the underlying data series, and is used to identify each curve when there are many others on the page.
Showing	Whether the curve should be drawn on the graph.
Show Line	Whether to draw a line connecting each data point.
Line Width	The width of the connecting line, measured in pixels.
Line Pattern	The line pattern to use. A list of possibilities is provided in a drop-down box.
Show Symbols	Whether to draw symbols at each data point
Symbol Size	The diameter of the symbols in pixels
Symbol Type	The type of symbol to draw. Any symbol other than a Square or Single Pixel is drawn as a square on the screen and drawn correctly in PostScript output. A list of possibilities is provided in a drop-down menu.
Color	The color of the curve. A list of possibilities is provided in a drop-down menu. The last choice is "Other..." which displays a dialog box for choosing a color. By clicking a tab at the top of the dialog, the color may be specified by picking it from an array of color cells, in Hue-Saturation-Brightness (HSB) format, or in Red-Green-Blue (RGB) format.

To use the Properties Dialog to create the changes in *figure 9*, the user would expand the tree to show the *Graph* nodes, and then select the first curve within the last showing graph and change *Line Pattern* from "Solid" to "Dashed" and *Color* from "Green" to "Yellow". Select the second curve and change *Line Pattern* from "Dashed" to "Solid" and *Line Width* from "1" to "3". Select the third curve and uncheck the *Show Line* check box, check the *Show Symbols* check box, change *Symbol Type* to "Hollow Circle", and change *Symbol Size* to "7". Finally, change *Color* to "Other…" and specify an RGB value of (24, 213, 255).

Data-series objects store multidimensional data, and appear in the form of *DataSeries*, *XyDataSeries*, or *TimeSeries* objects. Each contains one child *Dimension* object for each of the dimensions. Each series' properties include:

Title	The name of the series used to keep track of it among the others.
Number of Dimensions	The number of dimensions stored in the series. This is for the user's information and is not editable.
Number of Points	The number of points stored in the series. This is for the user's information and is not editable.
Number of Points Selected	The number of points in the series that currently are selected for modification. This is for the user's information and is not editable.

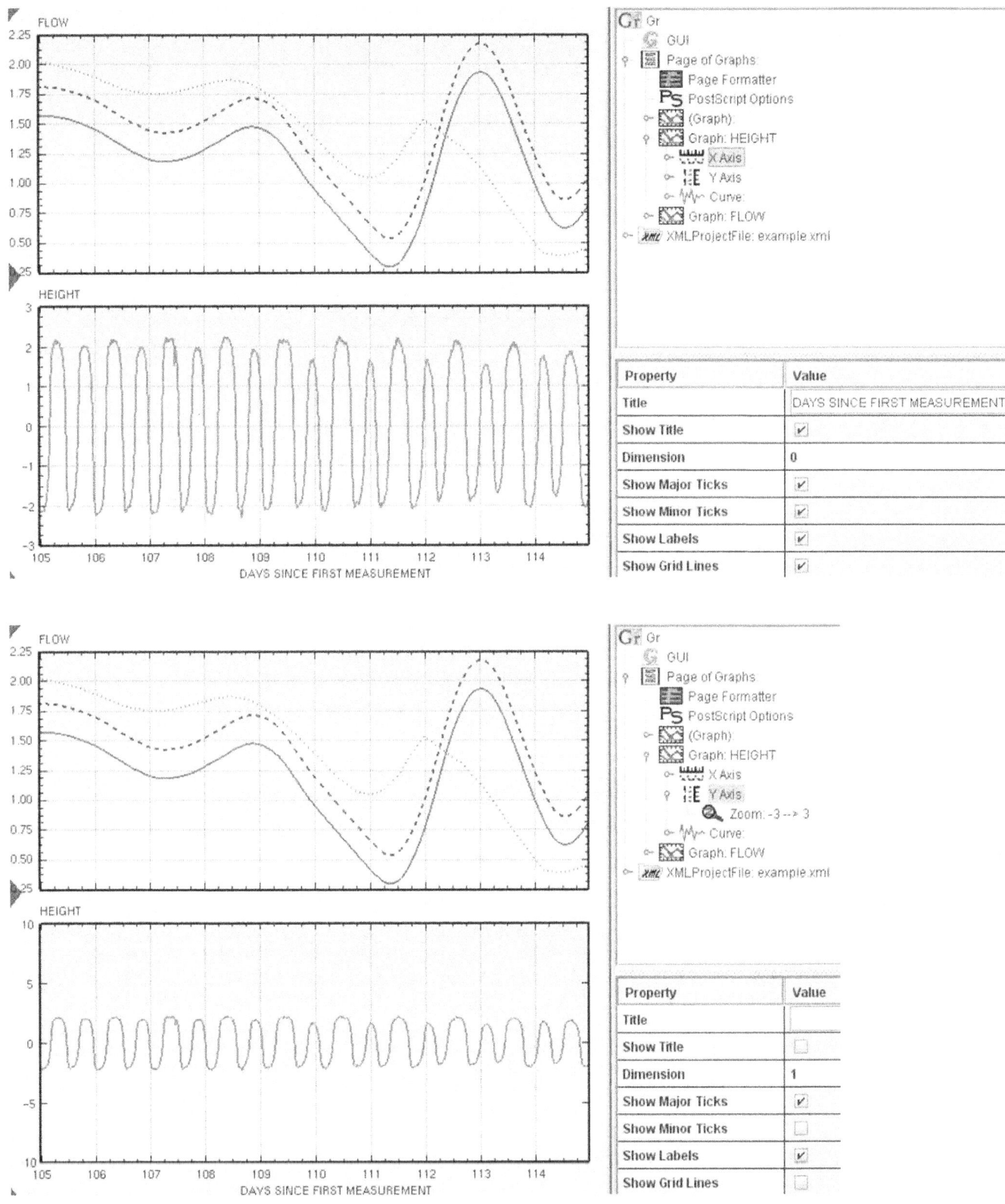

Figure 8. The Gr Application, showing certain axis properties and the accompanying graphs. Changes were made to the properties in (A) to create (B), and axis range and tick spacing properties then were changed to create (C).

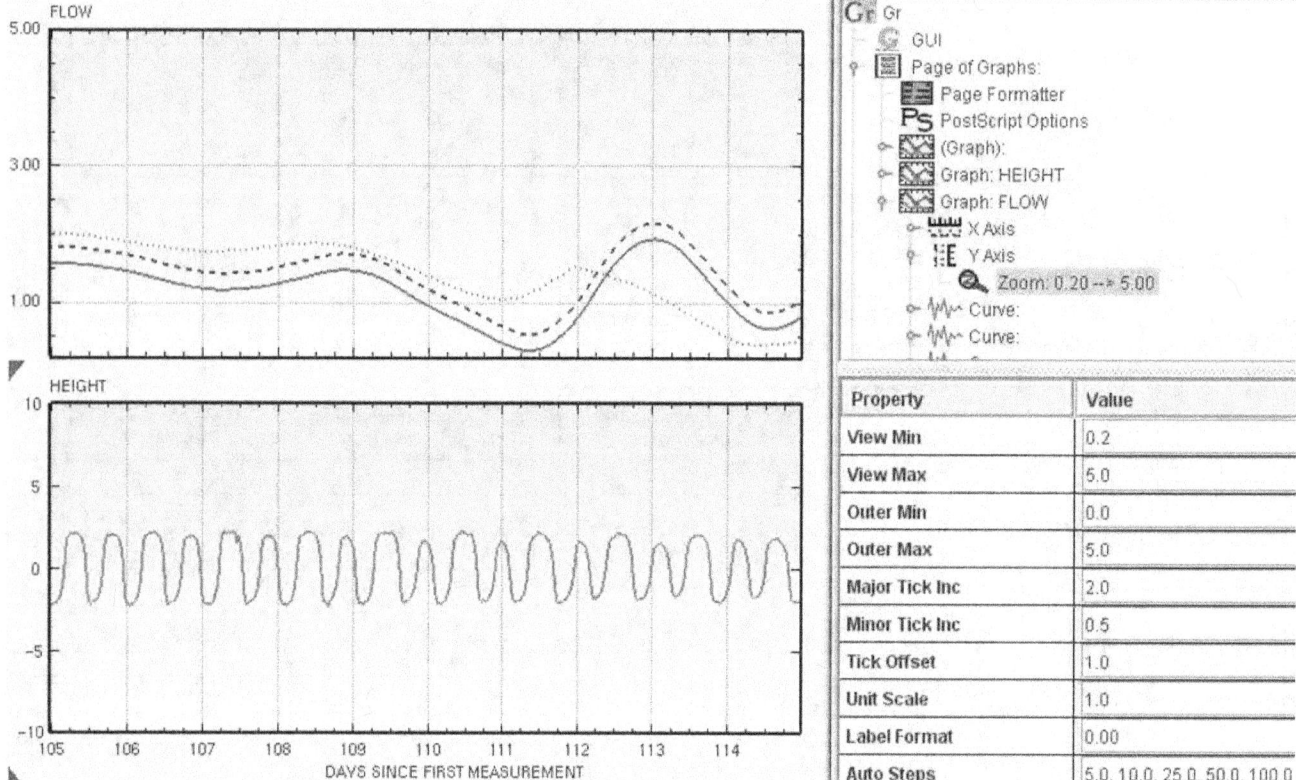

Figure 8.   Continued.

TimeSeries objects have all the properties of *XyDataSeries* objects with the additional property:

Reference Year	The year from which all time dimensions are referenced.

A *Dimension* object describes and controls one dimension of a data series, such as the X dimension. It has the following properties:

Title	The name of the series used to keep track of it among the others.
Number of Dimensions	The number of dimensions stored in the series. This is for the user's information and is not editable.
Number of Points	The number of points stored in the series. This is for the user's information and is not editable.
Number of Points Selected	The number of points in the series that currently are selected for modification. This is for the user's information and is not editable.

Modes

Typically Gr operates in one of three modes—*Pan*, *Zoom*, or *Select*—which are displayed as the selected radio button (*fig. 10*). The current mode can be changed by clicking on one of the other radio buttons. To learn how each mode functions, see the sections of this manual on Zooming and Panning, and also on Selecting and Dragging Data Points.

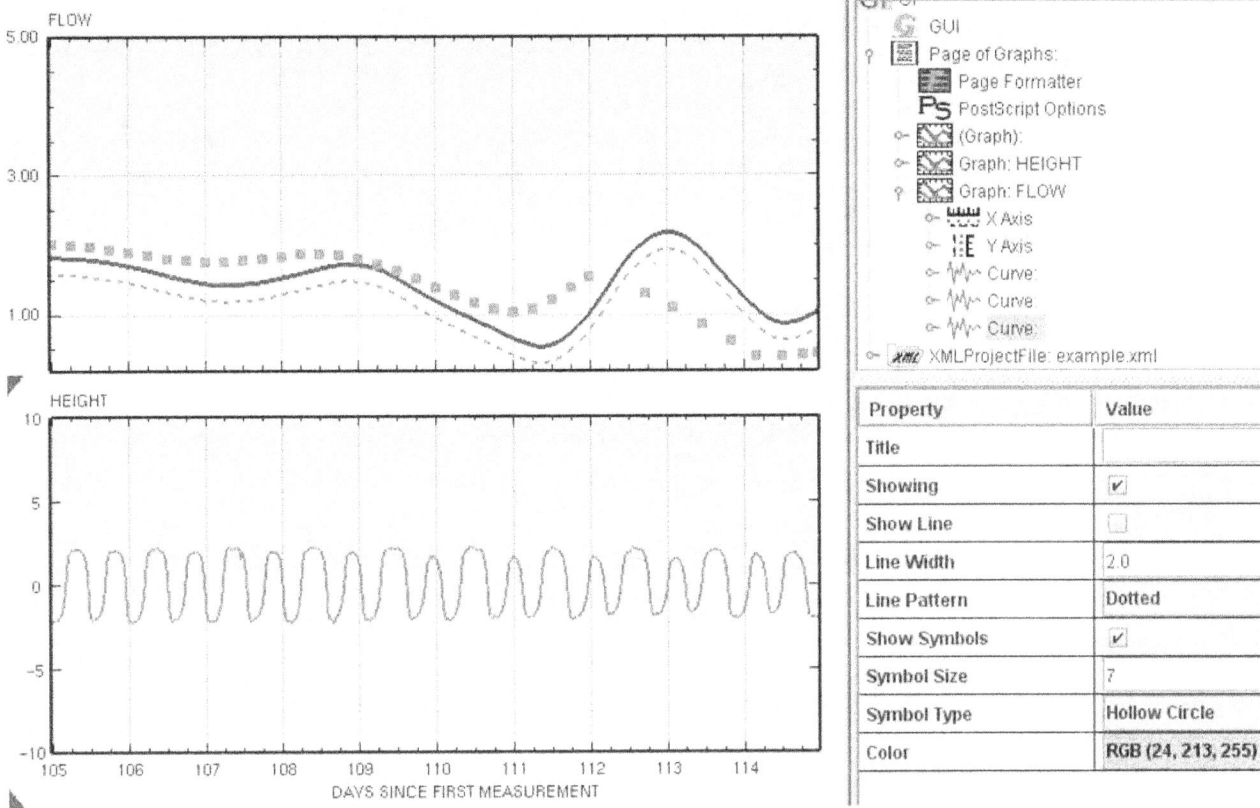

Figure 9.   Example of properties for each graph shown in the Properties Dialog box, and curves that have been modified within the top graph in the Gr Application.

Zooming and Panning

The mouse can be used to zoom in and pan around each graph. With each zoom in or out, the tick and label increments for each axis are recalculated to suitable values. These values are determined partially by the size of the Gr window. Therefore, resizing the window can change the tick and label increment values.

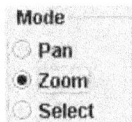

Figure 10.   Example of the Mode Panel box that uses radio buttons to indicate the current mode in the Gr Application.

Zooming with the Mouse

To zoom in on a graph, hold down the Shift button, and move the mouse to the corner of the area to be examined. With the Shift button down, press and hold either the left or right mouse button as the mouse is dragged to the opposite corner of the area to be zoomed and released. A dashed rectangle trails the mouse cursor, but it isn't necessary to wait for it to completely size to the mouse cursor location (*fig. 11*). Gr will use the position of the mouse cursor—not the dashed, selection rectangle—to determine the corner of the zoom window. Depress the Shift key until the zoom operation is completed.

To zoom in without using the Shift button, click the *Zoom* radio button within the *Mode* panel on the toolbar. Then define the zoom window with the mouse the same way that is described in the previous paragraph. Once the zoom operation is completed, Gr automatically will switch to *Pan* mode.

If a zoom window is drawn that spans more than one graph, the zoom request will be ignored. If the zoom window is completed properly, the major and minor tick increments will be adjusted so that a similar number of labels always are present along each axis. The increments used are 10, 25, 50, or one of these numbers multiplied by a power of 10, such as 0.25 or 500.

Zoom Commands

To zoom in a set amount on all selected graphs, select *Zoom In* (Ctrl+Shift+Z, think "Big Z") from the *View* menu. To zoom out a set amount, select *Zoom Out* (Ctrl+Z, think "Little Z") from the *View* menu. To zoom out to show the contents of the graph, choose *Zoom All* (Ctrl+L) from the *View* menu. The contents of each graph are reviewed during *Zoom All*, so if curves are edited and span more or less area than before, the zoom boundaries will be updated to reflect the latest edits. The zoom operations affect all axes belonging to selected graphs. Usually, the X axis is shared among all graphs.

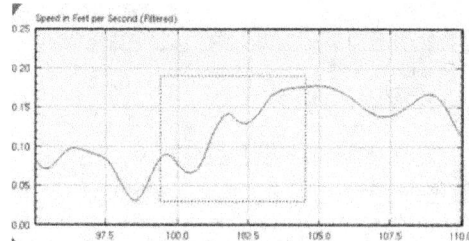

Figure 11.   An example of an area selected for zooming within a graph in the Gr Application.

As long as the image is not zoomed out completely, it is possible to pan around by pressing and holding either the left or right mouse button and dragging it. It also is possible to pan by holding down the Ctrl key and pressing one of the arrow keys on the keyboard (left, right, up, or down). This action causes all graphs on the screen to pan the length of one major tick mark in the direction of the arrow. It is not possible to pan (or zoom out) past the outer min or max. When the *Zoom All* command is given, the view min and max are set to be the same as the outer min and max.

The Status Bar

A status bar containing information about the page is along the bottom of the Gr window. When Gr is first started, it displays the Default Status Bar, which contains a minimal set of GUI components (*fig. 12*) that is simple and easy to understand. Optionally, the Detailed Status Bar can display more information and allow the user to edit the properties of curves on the page.

The Default Status Bar

The leftmost component on the Default Status Bar is a button labeled < *More* > that allows the user to switch to the Detailed Status Bar. Next to this button are two text fields containing the coordinates of the point with an X value nearest that of the mouse cursor. The X coordinate is on the left and the Y coordinate is to its right. As the mouse cursor is moved around the graph, these numbers are updated automatically.

Figure 12.   The Default Status Bar, as shown in the Gr Application.

If the X coordinate is a date and time, it can be written in a number of different formats. Holding down the Ctrl key and clicking on the X coordinate label will cycle through the available formats (*fig. 13*). When the mouse is clicked with the cursor over a label, the label format descriptor is displayed, but if the mouse cursor then is moved over a time-series curve, the label will show an actual date. If the mouse is moved over a curve that does not represent a time series, the default label format will be displayed.

Another important piece of information displayed on the status bar is the current mode: *Pan, Zoom, Select,* or *Drag.* If Gr is in *Select* or *Drag* modes, the left mouse button is reserved for other operations, and the right button must be used to pan or zoom. Clicking the *Pan* radio button, or selecting it from the *View* menu (Ctrl+Shift+X), will enable the *Pan* mode from any of the other three modes. Clicking the *Zoom* radio button will enable the *Zoom* mode, which allows a zoom window to be drawn without holding down the Shift key.

Gr can lock in place the X or Y axes so they are not affected by zoom or pan operations. To toggle the locks, choose *Lock X* (Ctrl+Alt+X) or *Lock Y* (Ctrl+Alt+Y) from the *View* menu. The status bar at the bottom of the Gr window has two buttons that show whether or not the axes are locked. These buttons can be clicked to toggle the locks. On the default status bar, these buttons are labeled *X Locked* or *X Unlocked* and *Y Locked* or *Y Unlocked.*

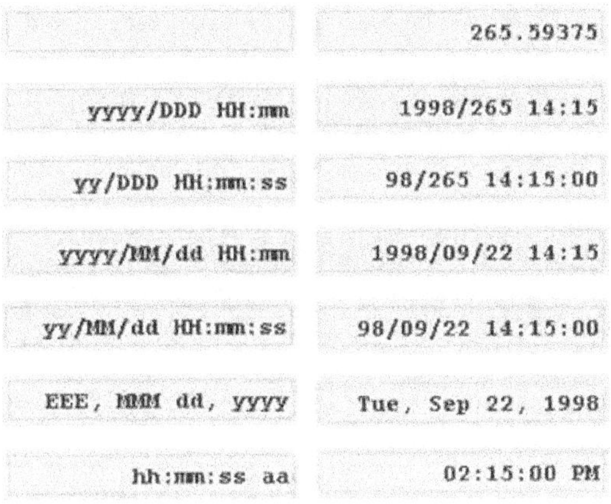

Figure 13. Available format descriptors (left column) and their respective outputs (right column), as shown in the Gr Application.

The Detailed Status Bar

The Detailed Status Bar contains the information found on the Default status bar as well as additional information and features (*fig. 14*). Clicking the < *More* > button on the Default Status Bar displays this feature. Clicking the > *Less* < button will switch back to the Default Status Bar.

The Detailed Status Bar is organized into four panels of GUI components. The first panel contains a box labeled *Choose Curve* that lets the user choose the event that will cause the status bar to be updated with the curve information that is nearest the mouse cursor (*fig. 15*). The first choice is *Under Mouse* and causes the status bar to be updated each time the mouse is moved within the graph area. The second choice is *With Click* and causes the status bar to be updated each time the user clicks the mouse within the graph area.

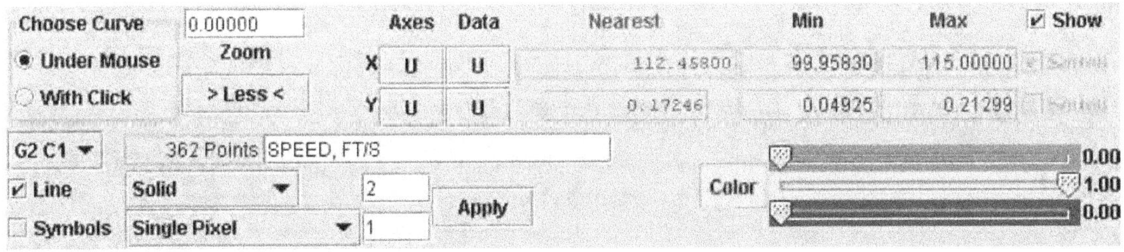

Figure 14. The Detailed Status Bar, as shown in the Gr Application.

There are three other components on the first panel. Two of these are the > *Less* < button and the mode indicator, which previously have been described in this report. The remaining component is a text field that describes the format specification used for displaying the coordinates of points. The format specification follows the convention of `java.text.Decimal-Format,` as described under the Label Format entry of the Properties Dialog. The default format specification is 0.00000. This format specification affects the appearance of all coordinates on both the Detailed and Default status bars.

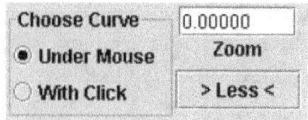

Figure 15.   Panel 1 of the Detailed Status Bar, as shown in the Gr Application.

The second panel is arranged as a table with three rows (*fig. 16*). The top row consists mostly of column headings. The middle row is for the X dimension and the bottom row is for the Y dimension. The leftmost column consists of the row labels *X* and *Y*. The column immediately to its right, under the *Axes* heading, has two toggle buttons labeled either *L* or *U*, for Locked or Unlocked, which are used to lock or unlock the X or Y axes. Under the *Data* column, there are two more buttons of the same type that lock or unlock the X or Y dimensions of the chosen data series for editing. The default setting is for the X dimension to be locked and the Y dimension to be unlocked. This allows points to be dragged up and down without affecting their position along the X axis.

The next column is labeled *Nearest* and shows the coordinates of the nearest point to the mouse cursor, as of the last update. These are the same as the coordinates shown on the Default Status Bar. Next is a column labeled *Min*, which shows the smallest X and Y coordinates in the chosen series. Beside it is a column labeled *Max*, which shows the largest X and Y coordinates in the series.

	Axes	Data	Nearest	Min	Max	☑ Show
X	U	U	112.45800	99.95830	115.00000	☑ Sorted
Y	U	U	0.17246	0.04925	0.21299	☐ Sorted

Figure 16.   Panel 2 of the Detailed Status Bar, as shown in the Gr Application.

The rightmost column consists of three check boxes. The top check box allows the user to show or hide the chosen curve. This can be useful when a curve is obscuring other curves and is making it difficult to see or select points on the other curves. If a curve is hidden, it cannot be chosen by clicking on it or moving the mouse over it. To show a curve after it has been hidden requires that it must be selected, which can be done using the curve list choice box in the third panel of the status bar.

The two check boxes below the *Show* check box are disabled permanently and used only for information. The check boxes inform the user whether the X and Y dimensions of the chosen data series are sorted in ascending order. A typical curve will be sorted in the X dimension and unsorted in the Y direction. If the X dimension is unsorted, the curve cannot be chosen by moving the mouse cursor over it or clicking on it. If the status bar appears to be ignoring a curve, that may be the reason. You still can choose the curve using the curve list choice box.

The third panel on the Detailed Status Bar is arranged as three rows of components (*fig. 17*). The curve list choice box in the top left corner lists all the curves on the page, including hidden curves and curves on hidden graphs. The curves are described according to their index number within their graph and according to their graph's index number within the page. For example, the third curve on the second graph is listed as "G1 C3".

To choose a curve from the curve list, click on the box and a list will pop up or down, depending on the proximity to the box margins. If the list of curves is long, it may have a scroll bar along the side to view all of the items. If there is sufficient space below the box, the list will pop down. If there is not, it may pop up over the graph area. If the list pops up and covers the graph area, it may be best to use the *With Click* option in the *Choose Curve* box so that your selection from the curve list will not be changed immediately when you move the mouse cursor within the graph area.

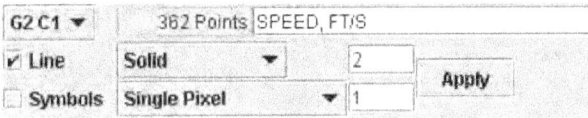

Figure 17.   Panel 3 of the Detailed Status Bar, as shown in the Gr Application.

A text field displaying the number of points in the chosen data series is on the top row next to the curve list. To the immediate right is an editable text field containing the title of the chosen series. The title can be edited the same way as in the Properties Dialog and by clicking *Apply* when finished.

The middle row of the third panel contains three components describing the line connecting the data points of the chosen series. The check box can be used to activate or deactivate the line. The choice box beside the check box gives several options for the line type, and the text field is used for changing the width of the line. The default width is a value of one. The line on the screen may differ from the PostScript output.

The bottom row describes the symbols that are drawn at each data point in the chosen series. The check box can be used to activate or deactivate symbols. The choice box provides a choice of which type of symbol should be used and the text field provides a choice for setting the size of the symbols. The default diameter on the screen is five pixels and five points on the printed output. All symbol types are drawn as filled squares on the screen, but they are drawn correctly on the PostScript output. Since the *Single Pixel* symbol is no wider than a line, it is drawn larger on the screen when the line is activated.

The fourth panel on the Detailed Status Bar contains three slider bars for changing the intensity of the RGB color of the chosen curve (*fig. 18*). The top slider controls the amount of red, the middle slider controls the amount of green, and the bottom slider controls the amount of blue. The numbers to the right give the level of each color as a number between 0.00 and 1.00. The resulting color is displayed to the left of the sliders. If PostScript output is desired, colors on the PostScript output must be enabled in the Properties Dialog and are darkened automatically from their onscreen appearance. Information on creating colors using RGB sliders is in *Appendix C*.

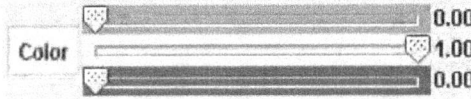

Figure 18.   Panel 4 of the Detailed Status Bar, as shown in the Gr Application

Selecting and Dragging Data Points

Each curve on the screen is a series of data points connected by straight line segments. Points may be selected with the mouse either individually or in groups. Mouse selection allows moving or deleting points. Once changes are made Gr allows each curve's data series to be edited and the changes saved to a file.

Selecting Points

To select points, first enter *Select* mode by clicking the *Select* radio button on the toolbar, or choosing it from the *Edit* menu (Ctrl+Shift+S). This causes every point on the currently selected graph to be drawn as a small, filled square, several pixels in diameter. For curves with many points, this command appears to increase the line weight of the curves, however, zooming in will reveal thin line segments connecting the individual points. The right mouse button must be used to pan or zoom while in *Select* mode.

To select a point, move the tip of the mouse cursor somewhere over the filled square that marks the point and click the left mouse button. Once the point is selected, it will change color (*fig. 19*). Care should be taken to not drag the mouse when the button is down if the intention is to select only one point. If difficulty arises using this selection technique, the selection window may be a better option, as described below.

Multiple points can be selected by drawing a rectangle from corner to corner, similar to drawing a zoom window. To do this, move the mouse cursor so that it does not cover any points and it is in the corner of the selection area. Press the left mouse button, drag the mouse cursor to the opposite corner of the selection area, then release the button. The first curve in the first graph, with points within that area, will have those points selected. All other points are deselected.

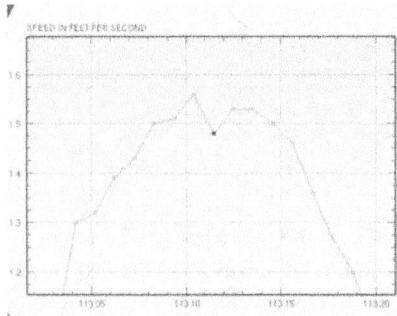

Figure 19. An example of a Selected Point in a graph, as shown in the Gr Application.

To add to the selection, hold down the Ctrl key and drag a selection box around the new selection area. Only points on the selected curve will be selected. To select points on other curves, hold down the Shift key. This allows the selection of points on all curves within the selection area, and the area is allowed to span across multiple graphs. Holding down Ctrl and Shift together adds more points to the selection from every curve within the selection area. To deselect an area, hold down the Alt key and draw a selection rectangle. If the rectangle spans multiple graphs, the Shift key will have to be held down to deselect points on all the graphs. The keyboard modifiers work the same way with single points; click one point at a time instead of drawing a selection rectangle.

To quickly select all the points on curves that are selected partially, choose *Select All* (Ctrl+A) from the *Edit* menu. To deselect all points on the page, choose *Deselect All* (Ctrl+D) from the edit menu.

Deleting Points

To delete the points that are selected, press the Delete key on the keyboard. Alternately, click the *Delete* button under the *Selection* heading on the toolbar or select *Delete* from the *Edit* menu. The deleted points will appear as cyan marks just outside the top of the graph's frame. Those marks appear only in *Select* or *Drag* modes and are used to indicate where data have been deleted or are missing. Sometimes deleted points are marked before deletions are made. This can happen if the data file that was opened contained deleted points. All data files cannot be relied on to list points that have been deleted and, by default, Gr does not save deleted points. If all the points in a curve are deleted, the two endpoints will be restored automatically, so the curve still can be selected.

If any curve is completely empty, its endpoints are restored automatically with Y values of zero. This allows the ends to be selected and the interior points to be restored. To delete these curves, use the *Cut* command as described under "Copying Curves and Undoing Operations."

Dragging Points

To interactively change the Y coordinates of the selected points, hold down Ctrl and move the mouse over one of the selected points. Press the left mouse button, drag the mouse up or down by the desired amount, and then release the mouse button. Horizontal motion is ignored while dragging points as long as the X dimension of the data series is locked. A shortcut for dragging a single point that is not selected is to simply move the mouse cursor over it, press the left mouse button, then drag the point to a new location. No keys are required to be held down, and all previously selected points will be deselected before the point is moved.

The Modify Dialog

Once points have been selected, many actions can be applied to them. The most basic actions are grouped together in the *Modify Selected Points* dialog box (Modify Dialog) (*fig. 20*). To open the dialog, click the *Modify* button on the toolbar or select it from the *Edit* menu (Ctrl+M). It is a modal dialog box, like the Properties Dialog, so the main Gr window cannot receive input until it is closed. Also, like the Properties Dialog, there is an *Apply* button present.

Pressing *Apply* applies the action to the main window and leaves the dialog open so other actions can be applied to the same selection. Pressing *Close* closes the window without changing the selected points.

The two other buttons are *Undo* and *Redo*. They provide the use of the *Undo* and *Redo* commands from the Modify Dialog.

Choosing an Operation

The top left area of the Modify Dialog is entitled *Operation* and has two groups of components that can be used to specify actions that can be taken on the selected points. The first *Operation* group is made up of six radio buttons:

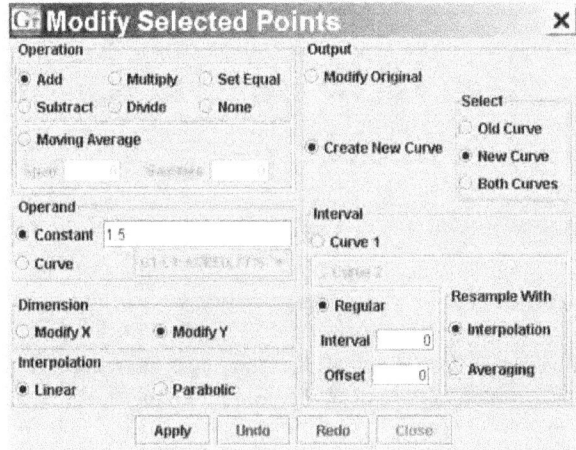

Figure 20.   The Modify Dialog window, as shown in the Gr Application.

Add	Adds a user-specified number to every selected point
Subtract	Subtracts a user-specified number from every selected point
Multiply	Multiplies every selected point by a user-specified number
Divide	Divides each selected point by a user-specified number
Set Equal	Sets every selected point equal to a user-specified number
None	Leaves each selected point unchanged. None can be used with some of the output options to resample a curve without otherwise changing it

The default action is *None*.

The second *Operation* group is an alternate choice to the six operators in the first *Action* group. This group is called *Moving Average*, and it has two associated text fields:

Span	The span of the moving average
Samples	The number of equally spaced samples that will be taken over by the span.

Unlike the other operators, the moving average is applied to all points on any curve that has points selected. An area equal to half the span will be deleted from both ends of the curve after the average is applied.

The *Operand* group contains two choices for the operand to be used with the operator chosen from the first *Action* group. If *Constant* is selected, you can type a number into the text field beside it. If *Curve* is selected, however, the operand will be an entire curve. To specify a curve as the operand, *Y Dimension* must be selected in the second *Action* group. The curves are listed according to their index within their graph, and their graph's index on the page. Each curve listed has the letter "G" followed by the index of its graph, the letter "C" followed by the index of the curve within the graph, and the title of the curve that was assigned when it was created.

The value of a curve operand at any given point on the X axis is the Y value of the curve at that point. The method used to determine that Y value can be picked from the *Interpolation* area at the bottom left of the Modify Dialog. When using a curve for the operand, if any selected points have X values lower than the operand curve's defined X range, then all points on the output curve below that range will be deleted. Similarly, if there are selected points with X values greater than the operand curve's X range, all points on the output curve above that range will be deleted.

The *Dimension* group is made up of two radio buttons:

Modify X	Causes the X coordinate of each selected point to be modified, and
Modify Y	Causes the Y coordinate of each selected point to be modified.

Modify Y is the default. The *Modify X* option is disabled if the chosen operand is a curve, or if the operation is set to *None* or *Moving Average*.

Interpolation

The *Interpolation* box in the lower left corner of the Modify Dialog has two radio buttons: *Linear* and *Parabolic*. They are used to specify which method to use when determining the Y value of a curve at a given point on the X axis. The added point may be between the data points that define the curve, which means the value must be interpolated. Picking linear interpolation will cause Gr to fit a straight line between the two nearest points and use the Y value of the line at the specified point on the X axis (*fig. 21*).

Picking parabolic interpolation will cause Gr to fit one parabola through the two nearest preceding points and the nearest following point, and a second parabola through the nearest preceding point and the two nearest following points. The Y values of the two parabolas at the specified point are averaged to arrive at the Y value that will be used. Some curves will be more accurately interpolated with the linear method while others, such as a sine wave, would be better interpolated using the parabolic method.

Output

The right half of the Modify Dialog is devoted to options related to the output of the specified operation. At the top of the *Output* area are two radio buttons that allow the output to be created as a new curve (*Create New Curve*), or written over the

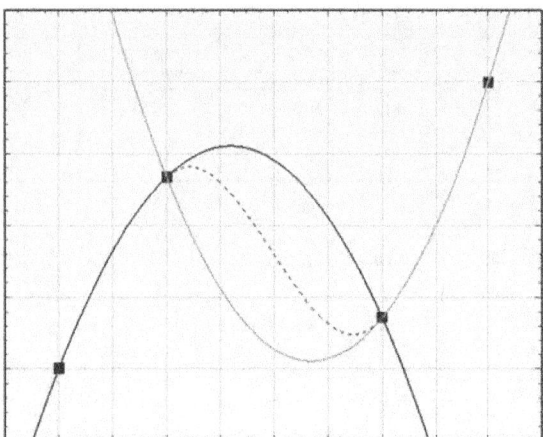

Figure 21.   An example of two parabolas (solid lines) fitted through four points and averaged to find the solution (dashed line) that is used with parabolic interpolation in the Gr Application.

original curve (*Modify Original*). *Modify Original* is the default choice. If you choose *Create New Curve*, you also will need to specify which curves should retain the selected region. The choices are presented in a radio button group labeled *Select*. They are *Old Curve*, which keeps the same points selected while creating a new curve with no selected points; *New Curve*, which deselects the old points but selects those same points on the new curve; and *Both Curves*, which keeps the same points selected and also selects those points on the new curve.

Currently, there is a software bug that arises when using *Create New Curve* with *Undo* and *Redo* causing Gr to lose the selected points. Also, selecting *New Curve* or *Both Curves* with any output interval other than *Curve 1* can cause the wrong points to be selected on the new curve.

The *Interval* area describes the spacing interval of points in the output. The default is *Curve 1* which means that points will be written with the same X values as points in the selected curve. If a curve is selected as the operand for the action, then *Curve 2* becomes an option for the output interval. Using this option will cause points to be written with the same X values as points in the operand curve.

The last interval choice is *Regular*, which writes regularly spaced points. You must enter the spacing interval into the *Interval* text field using the units the data are stored in. The *Offset* text field tells Gr where to start writing points. For example, if the data are measured in minutes and the points should be written at 5, 15, and 25, and so on, the entered interval should be 10 and the entered offset should be 5.

If the data-series times are measured in days, the spacing interval can be entered using a convenient notation where d is used for days, h for hours, m for minutes, and s for seconds. For example, 12h would be interpreted as 12 hours, or 0.5 days. Another example is 1d6h5.5m would be interpreted as 1 day, 6 hours, 5 minutes, and 30 seconds.

Whenever an output interval other than *Curve 1* is chosen, the entire curve will be resampled. In the bottom right corner of the Modify Dialog two choices are under *Resample With*. The *Interpolation* choice uses the specified interpolation method to determine the Y values for each new point. The *Averaging* choice uses the Y values of the old curve's points whenever possible. There is very little difference between the two methods when resampling from coarsely to finely spaced data. In that case, each method uses the chosen interpolation method to arrive at the value of each new point. *Interpolate* would use the value at one point on the old curve, while *Average* would average the interpolated values at two or three equally spaced places along the old curve (*fig. 22*).

The two methods differ more when resampling from finely spaced data to coarsely spaced data. For example, if the old curve had a point placed every two units on the X axis (0, 2, 4, 6, and so on), and was being resampled to have a point every nine units, the new curve would have points at 0, 9, 18, 27, and so on, along the X axis (*fig. 23*). If *Interpolation* is chosen, the Y value of the new curve at X=9 would be calculated by interpolating the Y value of the old curve at X=9. If *Average* is chosen, and linear interpolation is on, the Y value at X=9 would be calculated using the trapezoidal rule with the exact Y values from

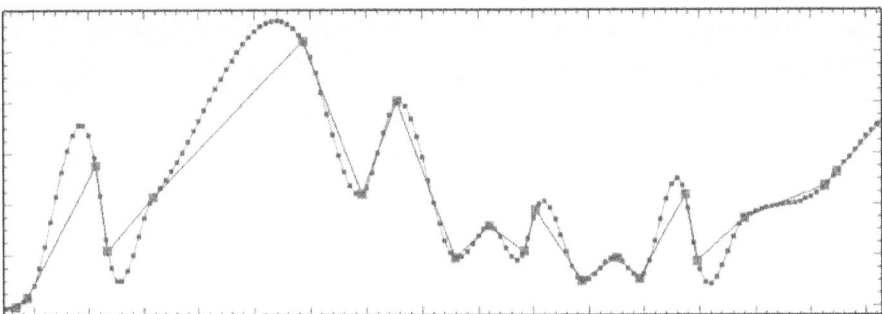

Figure 22. An example of resampling from a longer interval to a shorter interval using parabolic interpolation as shown in the Gr Application. The original curve is represented by the thicker line with larger points.

the points at X=6, 8, 10, and 12, and the interpolated values from X=4.5 and X=13.5. If parabolic interpolation is specified, the *Average* choice would average several equally spaced points along the curve between X=4.5 and X=13.5, with the end points receiving a half weighting. The Y values would be calculated at twice as many points across the span as there were in the old curve.

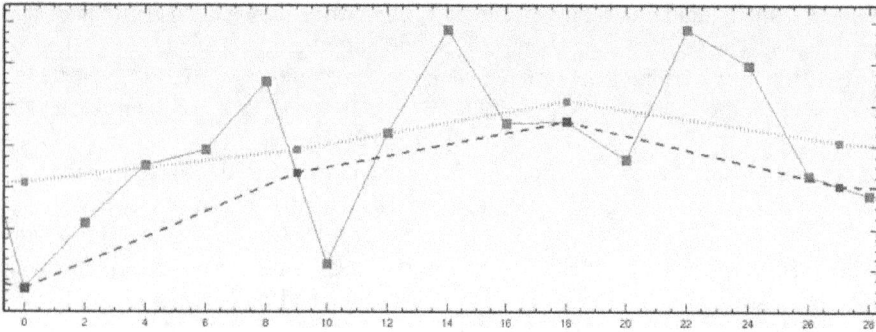

Figure 23. Resampling from an interval of two (solid line) to an interval of nine using linear interpolation (dashed line) and linear averaging (dotted line), as shown in the Gr Application.

Cutting, Copying, and Pasting Curves

Copies of curves can be made before modifying them by selecting any portion of the curve and then choosing *Copy* (Ctrl+C) from the *Edit* menu. This operation copies the entire curve to a buffer, overwriting the previous contents. If multiple curves are selected, they all will be copied. If no curves are selected when the command is given, the buffer remains unchanged. The *Cut* command (Ctrl+X) on the *Edit* menu works the same as *Copy* except the original curve is removed completely from the graph that contained it.

To paste the contents of the copy buffer, select the target graph or graphs, then choose *Paste* (Ctrl+V) from the *Edit* menu. The entire contents of the buffer will be pasted to each selected graph. The curves may have different line patterns or colors after they are pasted because each graph assigns the curve the next available pattern and color. The color and pattern of the new curve will depend on how many curves are already in the graph. The data in the new curves are not shared with the original curves, so each curve can be edited independently. Pasting can be used with the *New Graph* command to create multiple graphs with the same content. Clicking *Zoom All* will update the graph boundaries after cutting, pasting, or editing curves. The Properties Dialog enables cutting and pasting curves.

Undoing Operations

Most operations in Gr can be undone by choosing *Undo* (Ctrl+U) from the *Edit* menu. This includes cutting and pasting operations, the addition or deletion of graphs, and changes to a graph's properties. Selections cannot be undone, but any modification made to a selection can be undone, including changes made by dragging the mouse cursor or using the Modify Dialog. Gr supports multiple levels of undo, so giving the *Undo* command repeatedly will undo successive operations. Undone operations can be redone by choosing *Redo* (Ctrl+Shift+U) from the *Edit* menu.

Gr implements the *Undo* capability by making a copy of every selected curve's underlying data series in its entirety before editing operations are performed. If needed, Gr copies the page layout before changing curve, graph, or page properties. In this way, the restored state is exactly the same as it was before the operation was performed. The alternative to this method would be to go backwards by applying the inverse of the original operation to recreate the original state. Although this process would take less memory than storing multiple backup copies, it can introduce errors and for certain operations, such as filtering, there are no inverses.

The advantage to the way Gr handles Undo is that the user does not have to worry about making mistakes while editing, since *Undo* will restore the original data completely. The disadvantage to the way Gr handles Undo is that the computer could run low on memory because backup copies of each curve are stored, which is especially critical when editing long data series. For this reason, there is an option to specify the number of successive undo operations that will be saved. In the Properties Dialog under *GUI*, there is a property labeled *Levels of Undo* with a drop down box beside it. The choices are *0, 5, 10, 20, 40, 80,* and *unlimited*. The default is *20*. When fewer levels of undo are chosen, remember that all stored backups beyond that number will be deleted immediately from memory when a change is applied.

Gr keeps only one list of undoable operations, so layout changes are intermixed with edit operations. This means that if a point is moved, a graph is hidden, and a curve is pasted, undoing the movement of the point isn't an option until pasting the curve and hiding the graph are undone first. It is important to be aware of which operations can be undone to avoid confusion.

Tools

There are several miscellaneous commands under the *Tools* menu. Currently, they all either help fill gaps in or filter data series or reformat graphs. The tools that edit data work much the same way as tools in the Modify Dialog, and also can be undone.

Fillers and Filters

Gap fillers replace deleted points in a series. They work only with gaps whose deleted points are identified with cyan markers at the top of the graph. The new points have the same X values as the deleted points, but use calculated Y values. The two gap fillers are *Fill Gaps Linearly* (Ctrl+Shift+L) and *Fill Gaps Parabolically* (Ctrl+Shift+P). Both commands work similarly with the only difference being the appearance of the filled portion after execution. To use the gap fillers, select points on both sides of a gap before giving the fill command. The fillers will look for deleted points within the range of selected points and restore all of them back to the data series (*fig. 24*).

The linear gap filler uses the restored points to form a straight line between the nearest point before and after the gap. The parabolic gap filler fits a parabola through the two points preceding the gap and the two points after the gap, using the same method as described for parabolic interpolation in the Modify Dialog.

The filter tool that currently is on the *Tools* menu is *Godin Filter (Godin, 1972)*, which is used for filtering the tidal influence out of water data. To use it, first make sure the X units of the data are in days, then select any part of the curve to be filtered, and select *Godin Filter* from the menu (*fig. 25*). This filter resamples the data series to hourly increments, and then applies

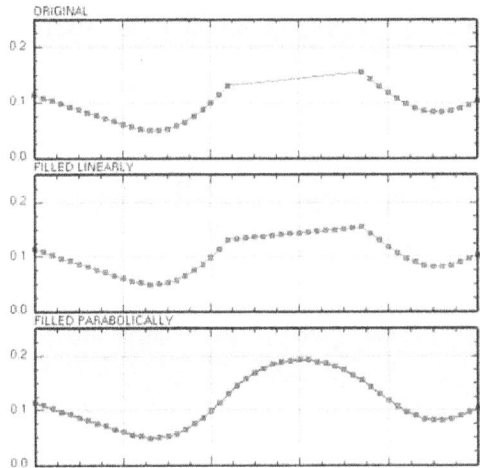

Figure 24.   Gap filling techniques for graphs in the Gr Application.

three passes. The first is a 12-1-11 hour moving average, using a 24-hour span with the averaged value written back to the 13th point of the span. The second pass takes the output of the first and applies an 11-1-12 hour moving average, using a 24 hour span with the averaged value written back to the 12th point of the span. The third pass is a 12-1-12 hour moving average, using a 25 hour span with the averaged value written back to the 13th point of the span. Approximately 1.5 days of data will be deleted from both ends of the data series (*fig. 26*).

The *Godin Filter* also can be used from the Properties Dialog. To do this, open the Properties Dialog, click on the *Gr* node, and right click to bring up the menu. Choose *Add New -> Tool -> Godin Filter*. Copy each of the *DataSeries* objects you would like to filter, click on the *Godin Filter* node and choose *Paste Original* from the right mouse menu. Next, click the *Apply* button, click on the *Godin Filter* node, and choose *Godin Filter -> Calculate* from the right mouse menu. Many *DataSeries* objects can be filtered at once with this method, but the filtering can't be undone as it can by using the *Tools* menu in the main Gr window.

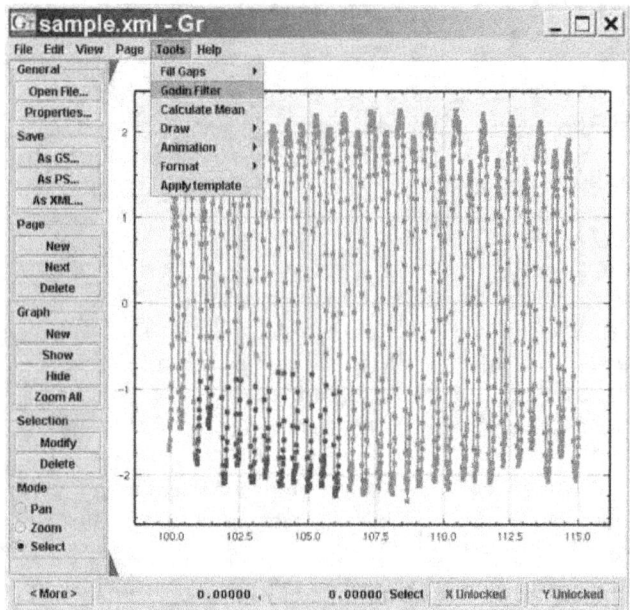

Figure 25.   Applying the Godin filter to a selected curve in a graph in the Gr Application.

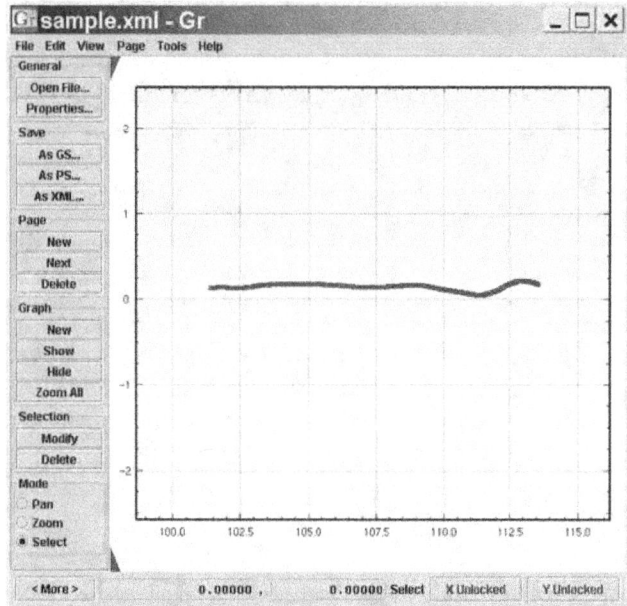

Figure 26.   The result of applying the Godin filter in a graph in the Gr Application.

Drawing New Curves

A new curve can be drawn by selecting *Start Drawing* (Ctrl+W) from the *Format* submenu of the *Tools* menu. Once the command is given, each mouse click within a graph is interpreted as the next point on the curve. To begin a new curve, give the *Start Drawing* command again. When finished drawing, select the *Stop Drawing* command (Ctrl+Shift+W) from the *Format* submenu of the *Tools* menu. A curve must have at least two points before it is shown. The *Undo* and *Redo* commands can be used to remove and restore the most recent points from the curve as it is drawn.

Page Formats

The format commands offer a way to quickly give plots a unique appearance on the screen or on the printed page. They also allow each user to work with the format that best suits them. Many of the changes made when applying a format also could be made using the Properties Dialog. Those changes can be modified further or undone using the Properties Dialog after applying a format. Formats also can add features to the plots that otherwise are not available, such as automatically numbering the graphs, or writing the current date. The format command may need to be given again after opening new files. If there is modification of curve or graph properties, such as line type or tick spacing, the format command may override those modifications.

The *Default Format* command is used to apply the default format to a page of graphs, usually after some other format has been applied. It deactivates any special features of the previous format, and returns all tick marks, grid lines, and graph titles to the default state.

The *Report Format* command is used for creating a page of graphs that would be suitable for use as figures in a USGS publication. When printed, the graphs would be the proper width and height, use Helvetica 8-point font, and proper line thickness. The *Report Format* command deactivates grid lines and minor tick marks on all graphs, hides the page and graph titles, and activates X and Y titles. The graphs on the screen are labeled A, B, C, and so on, and those labels are kept in order even when graphs are moved around. If time-series data are being viewed, the title is changed to read "DAYS FROM JANUARY 1," followed by the data's reference year.

The *Working Format* command adds extra information to the printed output of a page. The format uses landscape orientation and is similar to the default format. The date and time of the print is written in the upper left corner, and the full path names of all opened and overlaid files are written in the upper right corner. Also, deleted points are marked as hollow circles with an "X" through them. Most of these Working Format features only show up on printed output, with the exception being the current file, which is displayed on the screen as well as on the printed page.

The *Slide Format* command is used to generate a PostScript file that can be used as a slide in a presentation. The background is set to black with yellow graph lines and thick, colored curves. The PostScript font is set to 14-point Times-Bold-Italic.

Two additional formats are available by choosing them in the Properties Dialog under a page's *Formatter* property. *VariableSizeFormatter* allows each graph's height to be assigned an individual value. *VariableShapeFormatter* allows each graph's width, height, and position to be assigned fixed values individually.

Saving As XML

Gr's main format is based on Extensible Markup Language (XML). It is the only format Gr uses that can store data, page layout, and other program options in a single file. To save the current page, including all data series and hidden graphs, click the *As XML...* button under the *Save* heading on the toolbar, or select *Save As XML...* from the *File* menu. A dialog box will appear to enable naming the output file. The current page and its child objects will be written to that file. Use the *Open File...* command to open files saved in this manner.

Custom project files can be created that contain any number of pages or just data. To create the files, open the Properties Dialog, click on the *Gr* tree node, and right click to display the popup menu. Navigate through the *Add New* submenu, the *File* submenu, and select *XML Project File*. An empty XML file node will be added as a child of the *Gr* node. To add objects to the file, select them in the tree pane, copy them using the right mouse menu, then select the XML file node and choose *Paste Original* from the right mouse menu. Next, click the *Apply* button to send changes from the Properties Dialog to the actual Gr object hierarchy. Finally, select the XML file node, right click, and select *Save As...* from the *Gr File* sub menu. A dialog will appear to choose a file name, and then the file will be written to the disk.

Saving as GS Format

After changes have been made to data from a GS format file, they can be saved back to the same data file or to a new one. (See the GS Format section of Appendix A for more information about GS Format.) Click the *As GS...* button under the *Save* heading on the toolbar or select *Save As GS...* from the *File* menu (Ctrl+S). A dialog box will appear to specify the new file name. The default is the last file that was opened. After the file name is specified, click *Save* to save it or *Cancel* to close the dialog without saving. If a new file is saved over an existing file, a confirmation dialog must be answered before the file will be overwritten.

The file will be written in GS format and will include only curves from the most recently opened GS file. Curves that were opened in other formats, curves that were overlaid from other files in any format, or curves that were pasted onto the page will not be saved to the chosen file.

Printing

There is no true printing facility in Gr, but the image shown on the screen can be saved as a PostScript file (PS-Adobe-3.0, EPSF-3.0). That file can be sent directly to a PostScript printer or to a program such as GSView (*http://www.cs.wisc.edu/~ghost/*) to be viewed and printed. To create the PostScript file, click the *As PS...* button under the *Save* heading on the toolbar or select *Save As PS...* from the *File* menu (Ctrl+P). A dialog box will ask for the name of the print file.

When using the default format, the contents of the Gr window will be stretched to fit the page. Other formats vary in the way they fill the page. In most formats, deleted points are not marked on the PostScript output, even though they are shown on the screen. Rotated text, such as is shown on Y Axis titles, also looks different in print than on the screen. Gr cannot draw rotated text on the screen, therefore, it draws it the same as normal text. However, the text is properly rotated on the printed output.

The file that Gr creates emulates an Encapsulated PostScript (EPS) file when it is imported into another application, such as a word processor. Curves are drawn using rounded joints instead of mitered joints, which causes very jagged curves to be drawn more accurately by eliminating the tiny spikes that are apparent when rendering sharp, mitered corners. The difference is small but, sometimes, very noticeable.

By default, Gr attempts to reduce the number of points that are drawn. The algorithm that it uses eliminates points that are least likely to affect the appearance of the output by considering the horizontal and vertical scales at which the data will be plotted, and the width of the line that will connect the points.

Point reduction can be activated or deactivated in the Properties Dialog under the *PostScript Options* object. A check box to enable or disable point reduction is available for both lines and symbols. The *Line Reduction Tolerance* parameter is the distance, in line widths, that a line could be offset. For example, a width scale of 0.5 would indicate that it would be acceptable to skip any points that are within half the line's width of its exact location. The default conservatively is set to 0.25.

The Line Point Reduction (LPR) algorithm only eliminates points; it never adds, moves, or reorders points. The algorithm operates sequentially through the data series, eliminating consecutive points that are in line with each other. The algorithm eliminates more points from certain curves, such as those with gradual changes. It always plots the first and last points of the series (*figs. 27–30*).

The number of points in a *DataSeries can be reduced* independent of PostScript output by opening the mouse right-click menu in the Properties Dialog and choosing *Add New -> Tool -> Line Point Reducer*. Paste *DataSeries* objects into the tool, click *Apply*, and then choose *Line Point Reducer -> Calculate* from the right mouse menu. There are *X Scale*, *Y Scale*, and *Line Width* properties for the tool than can be modified before calculating a result. Remember, there is no undo capability when using tools within the Properties Dialog.

The Symbol Point Reduction (SPR) algorithm works in the same manner as the LPR algorithm, except that it checks to see if a given symbol is a sufficient distance from the last plotted symbol. The Symbol Reduction Tolerance parameter is measured as a proportion of the symbol's radius.

When the Debug Point Reduction box is checked, the user can see which points will be eliminated in the PostScript output. After activation, a PostScript file can be saved in the normal fashion. Zooming in on one of the curves will reveal which points were plotted. All the points are represented as small, magenta squares on the screen. The symbol points that were retained in the output are shown as medium yellow squares and the line points that were retained are shown as large cyan squares with a line connecting them.

The *Debug* setting can be used to experiment with the tolerance settings until it is determined which setting is most effective. When finished, simply uncheck the debug check box and the screen and PostScript drawing will return to normal.

The *Debug* setting causes the original PostScript output to be drawn first in red with no points eliminated. The reduced series are then plotted in a black overlay. This allows any differences between the two to stand out in red (*fig. 31*).

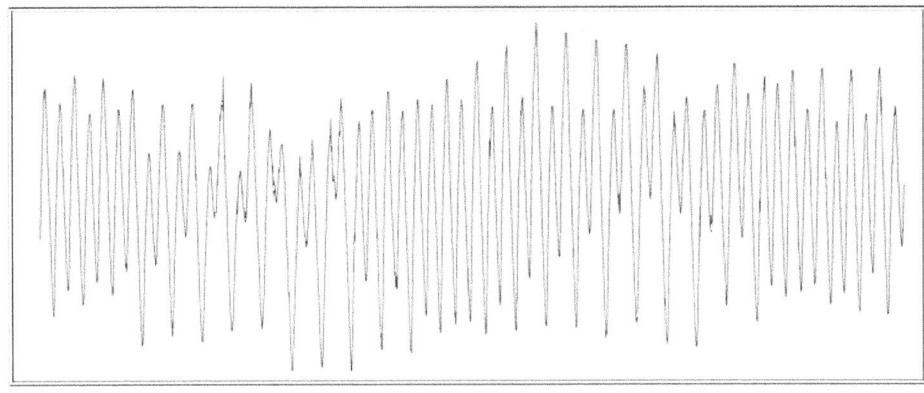

Figure 27.   The scale at which the graph was printed and at which the Line Point Reduction command is performed in the Gr Application. The curve shown contains 2,879 points.

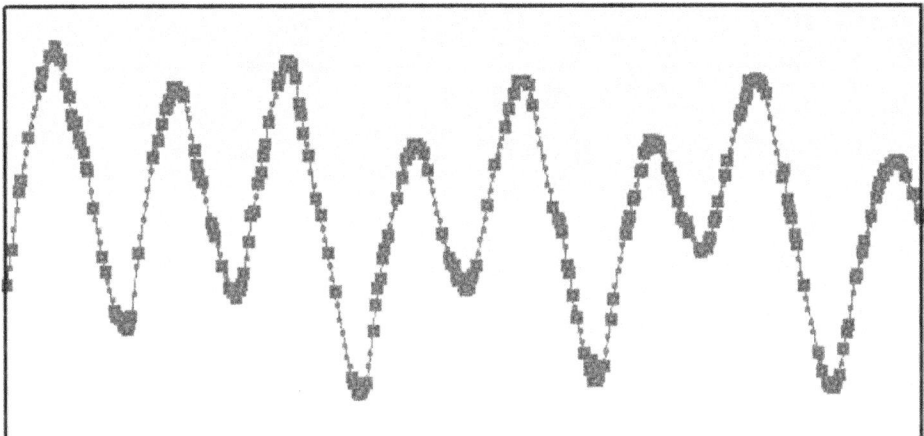

Figure 28.   Detail showing the points that were used to define the line with a Line Point Reduction width scale of 0.25, as shown in the Gr Application. Thick points represent points that were retained; this curve was reduced to 1,701 points.

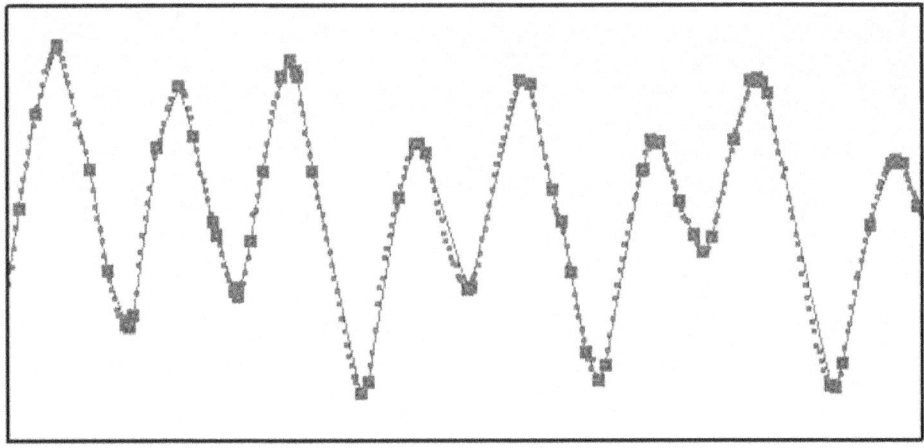

Figure 29.   Detail showing the points that were used to define the line with a Line Point Reduction width scale of 2.0, as shown in the Gr Application. Thick points represent points that were retained; this curve was reduced to 484 points.

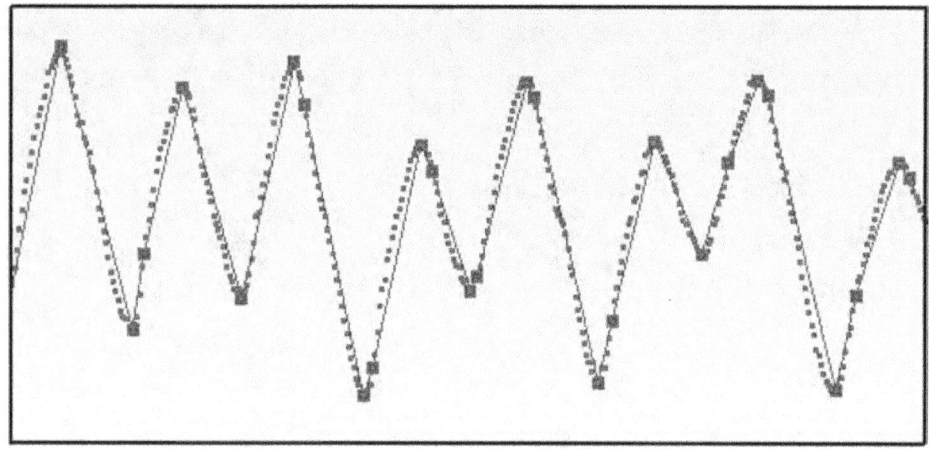

Figure 30. Detail showing the points that were used to define the line with a Line Point Reduction width scale of 10.0, as shown in the Gr Application. Thick points represent points that were retained; this curve was reduced to 44 points.

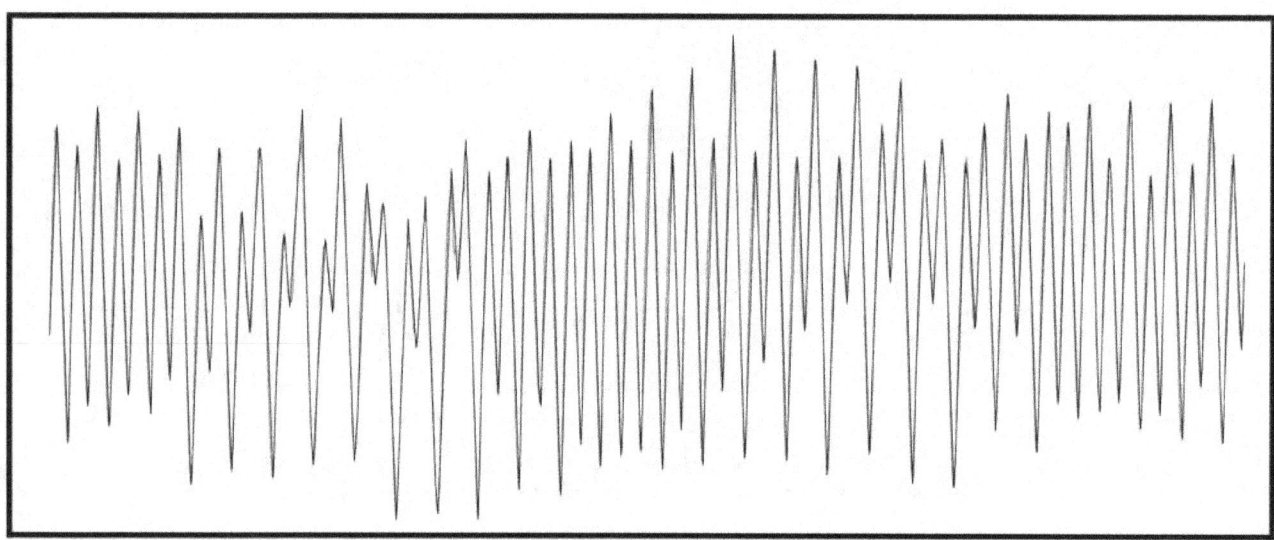

Figure 31. PostScript output of a black curve with a Line Point Reduction width scale of 10 over a red curve with Line Point Reduction width scale of 0, as shown in the Gr Application.

Templates

Editing graph properties to get the desired appearance can be one of the most time-consuming tasks performed with Gr. It can take 10 minutes to type in the axis limits, increments, labels, and titles for several graphs and to proofread them for errors. Afterward, it may be necessary to open another file and retype most or all of the same settings. To cut down on this effort, the user should save the appearance of a page and then apply it later as a template.

To create a template from an existing page, simply save it as an XML file. Then, open a new page of data and choose *Open XML Template...* from the *Page* menu. The properties of each object on the template page will be applied to the respective objects on the current page, without modifying the data. If there are more graphs or curves on the current page than in the template, Gr will cycle repeatedly through the template objects until all the objects on the current page have been updated. Extra objects in the template are ignored.

Apply Template on the *Tools* menu is another version of the *Open Template...* command on the *Page* menu. It is a shortcut for applying a template that already has been opened, after a new data file has been opened. It saves the effort of reselecting the same template file every time a new data file is opened.

There also is an *Open Classic Template...* command on the *Page* menu for opening the templates in the old Gr template format.

Summary

Gr can open X-Y data series from a file in one of several formats and present the data in variety of ways. The data can be shown as line or symbol plots in one or more vertically stacked graphs. The application represents the data as objects, and the user has the ability to modify the object properties in a table or by interacting directly with the graphs. Analysis can be performed by zooming and panning within the graphs or by applying one of the available data analysis tools. Data can be modified and saved to a data file or written to a PostScript file for printing.

References Cited

Adobe Systems, Inc., 1985, PostScript language tutorial and cookbook: Reading, Mass., Addison-Wesley, 243 p.

Adobe Systems, Inc., 1990, PostScript language reference manual: Reading, Mass., Addison-Wesley, 764 p.

California Department of Water Resources, California Department of Water Resources: accessed March 24, 2008, at URL http:// wwwdwr.water.ca.gov

Free Software Foundation, Inc., GNU lesser general public license: accessed March 24, 2008, at http://www.gnu.org/copyleft/ lesser.html

Godin, Gabriel, 1972, The analysis of tides: University of Toronto Press, Toronto, Ontario, Canada, 264 p.

JOGL, Welcome to the JOGL API Project!: accessed March 24, 2008, at https://jogl.dev.java.net/

Linux Online, Inc., The Linux home page at Linux Online: accessed March 24, 2008, at http://www.linux.org

Microsoft Corp., Microsoft: accessed March 24, 2008, at URL http://www.microsoft.com

National Oceanic and Atmospheric Administration, NOAA: accessed March 24, 2008, at http://www.noaa.gov

OpenGL.org, The industry's foundation for high performance graphics: accessed March 24, 2008, at http://www.opengl.org

Sun Microsystems, Inc., The source for Java developers: accessed March 24, 2008, at http://java.sun.com

Appendix A.   File Format Descriptions

Gr XML Format

The Gr XML format stores the Gr object hierarchy using standard XML syntax. For an explanation of XML, refer to *http://www.xml.com/pub/98/10/guide0.html* or other resources at *xml.com*. The main thing to remember is that all XML files use tags set off by < and > characters to describe a hierarchy of data. An element consists of everything between opening and closing tags such as `<tag attribute1="test"> element contents </tag>`. A single tag also can open and close an element, such as `<tag attribute1="test" />`. A simple XML file that defines an X-Y data series to Gr would be:

```
<?xml version="1.0"?>
<gov.usgs.gr>
 <dataseries numDimensions="2">
 10 10
 20 20
 30 20
 40 10
 50 50
 </dataseries>
</gov.usgs.gr>
```

The preceding file describes an object called *gov.usgs.gr* which has one child element called *dataseries*. The data series has one attribute that specifies the number of dimensions as "2" for X and Y. Inside the data-series element are data for five X-Y points. Notice that every element has an opening and closing tag.

When Gr writes out an entire page in XML format, each property of each object is written out. If these are not present when the file is read later, Gr assumes default values. Any part of the XML file can be edited by hand using an ASCII editor. An example of a Gr page written out in XML format is:

```
<?xml version="1.0" encoding="UTF-8"?>
<!-USGS Gr Version 2006-09-05->
<gov.usgs.gr>
 <obj class="gov.usgs.gr.visual.gl.PageOfGlGraphs" showTitle="false"
 title="simple.xml">
 <obj class="gov.usgs.gr.visual.PageFormatter"/>
 <obj class="gov.usgs.gr.visual.ps.PsOptions" LPR1WidthScale="0.25"
 SPRWidthScale="0.25" debugPointReduction="false" psColor="true"
 psColorBg="false" psFileName="gr.ps" psFont="Times-BoldItalic"
 psFontSize="12.0" psLandscape="true" psLineWidth="1.0" psSymbolSize="5.0"
 psUniformWidth="false" showPrintDialog="false"
 useLinePointReduction1="true" useSymbolPointReduction="true"/>
 <obj class="gov.usgs.gr.visual.gl.GlGraph" aspect1to1="false" show="true"
 showTitle="true" showXtext="true" title="Filtered Speed">
 <obj class="gov.usgs.gr.visual.gl.GlXAxis" dimension="0" showGridLines="true"
 showLabels="true" showMajorTicks="true" showMinorTicks="true"
 showTitle="false" title="">
 <obj class="gov.usgs.gr.visual.Zoom" labelFormat=" 0" majorTickInc="1.0"
 minorTickInc="0.25" outerMax="110.0" outerMin="0.0" tickOffset="0.0"
 unitScale="1.0" viewMax="110.0" viewMin="100.0"/>
 </obj>
 <obj class="gov.usgs.gr.visual.gl.GlYAxis" dimension="1" showGridLines="true"
 showLabels="true" showMajorTicks="true" showMinorTicks="true"
 showTitle="false" title="">
 <obj class="gov.usgs.gr.visual.Zoom" labelFormat="0.00" majorTickInc="0.25"
 minorTickInc="0.05" outerMax="100.0" outerMin="0.0" tickOffset="0.0"
```

```
unitScale="1.0" viewMax="1.0" viewMin="0.0"/>
</obj>
<obj class="gov.usgs.gr.visual.gl.GlCurve" color="Green" linePattern="Solid"
lineWidth="2.0" show="true" showLine="true" showSymbols="false"
symbolSize="5.0" symbolType="Single Pixel" title="">
<doubledataseries class="gov.usgs.gr.data.XyDataSeries" numDimensions="2"
numPoints="5" title="">
<doubledim class="gov.usgs.gr.data.DataDimension" locked="true" num="0"
snap="0.0" snapOffset="0.0" title=""/>
<doubledim class="gov.usgs.gr.data.DataDimension" locked="false" num="1"
snap="0.0" snapOffset="0.0" title=""/>
101 0.7675
102 0.4485
103 0.3507
104 0.5744
105 0.6603
</doubledataseries>
</obj>
</obj>
</obj>
</gov.usgs.gr>
```

Each element has a class attribute with the name of the Java class that Gr will use to represent the object within the program. The element hierarchy in the XML files exactly matches the tree node hierarchy in the Properties Dialog, and each element's attributes correspond with the values in the properties table.

GS Format

GS format is an ASCII time-series data format used by some USGS researchers. As a matter of convenience, Gr was written to easily read and write GS format; however, its use is not mandatory. GS format stores time-series data as a series of columns in plain text format. The file is divided into a header area at the beginning of the file and into a body area where the data values are given. There are several caveats in the way Gr reads and writes GS format that may be useful to know, even to the experienced GS user.

Reading the Header

The number of header lines varies, depending on the number of data series in the file. The header of a file with one series would be eight lines long, with each additional series adding a line to the header. GS files created by some programs contain extraneous characters at the ends of lines, including carriage-returns (CR). It is necessary to ignore these characters to count the number of lines in the header. Consequently, of the usual group of end-of-line indicators (CR, line feed [LF], and CR followed by LF), only LF is recognized in the header.

The official title that Gr gives the file is a combination of the entire first line of the file and the date read from the fourth line. Gr uses the file title as the page title by default. When the date is read from the fourth line of the header, Gr looks for four integer numbers separated by spaces, with extra spaces being ignored. The first is in columns 1–9 and represents the year. Gr can read a four-digit year or a two-digit year using a pivot year of 60. For example, a year of 60 would be interpreted as 2060, and 61 would be interpreted as 1961. The second number of the data is read from columns 10–12 and represents the month. The third number is read from columns 13–15 and represents the day. The fourth number is read from columns 16–20 and represents the hour and minute as a four-digit number. For example 1:35 p.m. would be given as 1335.

Gr ignores the rest of line four, including the start day, relative to January 1, 2000. The four numbers at the beginning of line four are used to determine the start day. Lines two, three, five, and six also are ignored. The number of channels, or data series, in the file is read from columns 41–46 on line four.

For each channel, an additional line containing the title, data type, and decimal offset is read. Gr reads these lines starting at line seven and continues reading until each channel's information has been read. The title is read as a character string from columns 3–22, the decimal offset is read as an integer from columns 23–28, and the data type index is read as an integer from columns 29–34. The title of each channel also is the title of the curve from which it is represented in Gr, and the first curve in each graph is used as the initial title of the graph. The decimal offset is used when reading data from the body of the GS file, and the data type is used to group curves of the same type on the same graph in Gr. After all the channel description lines have been read, one other line is read and ignored before the body is read.

Reading the Body

Each line in the body of the file has the time in the first column followed by the value of each series at that time in their respective columns. The time is given as the day of the year and decimal fraction of the day, all multiplied by 100,000. For example, January 1 at 00:00 would be written as 100000 and a non leap year, July 5 (day 186 of the year) at 11:15 p m. would be written as 18696875. This gives a time resolution of better than 1 second.

The lines in the body of the file are parsed as follows. Columns 1–9 are the date and time as described above. There is a six-space column for each channel with no space in between. Following those columns, there are four optional columns for displaying the date as year, month, day, and time. These columns are ignored by Gr when reading.

Writing GS Format

When writing data out to a GS file, Gr writes out the same header lines that originally were read; however, the body of the file contains new data. The original times are stored as integers so they can be written back at the same time steps that were read in. Missing values are written as 999999. If one or more of the channels has a point that is missing from the others, it is written at its own time step and the other channels are written as 999999. If all data are missing at a time step, that time step is not written to the file.

Here is a sample from the beginning of a GS file:

```
82130
 Max. spec. cond.: 39.7 ms., Min. sp. cond.: 17.8 ms.
start:-yr-mn-dy--hr----days-----dt-nchan-mxdig
 1994 1 5 1200 -2191 15.00000 6 6
 Station Latitude: 38 3 30 N, L Sensor depth (m below MLLW): #1=
ch------------name-digit-dtype-isens—ivec—iblg
 1salinity, ppt 1 5 1 0 0
 2salinity, ppt 1 5 2 0 0
 3temp. (degrees c) 1 6 1 0 0
 4temp. (degrees c) 1 6 2 0 0
 5spec. cond. ms/cm 1 8 1 0 0
 6spec. cond. ms/cm 1 8 2 0 0
---days-salin-salin-temp-temp-cond-cond—yr—mn—dy-hour
 570833 140 171 86 89 233999999 1994 1 5 1700
 571875 140 174 86 89 232999999 1994 1 5 1725
 572917 141 170 86 89 233999999 1994 1 5 1750
 573958 150 164 87 88 248999999 1994 1 5 1775
 575000 154 163 87 88 253999999 1994 1 5 1800
```

Other Data Formats

Besides GS format, there are several other formats available that can be parsed by Gr. They are organized within "packages", with the most common package being *gov.usgs.sfhydro.data*.

gov.usgs.gr.data.XyDataFile reads multiple space-delimited columns of X-Y data. The left-most column holds X data and all other columns hold Y data. There are no header lines.

Here is a sample of data in *XyDataFile* format:

```
 260.49 -164251.72
 260.50 -164367.70
 260.51 -162425.36
```

```
260.52 -159537.22
260.53 -155386.58
260.54 -151899.09
260.55 -147685.55
```

gov.usgs.gr.data.DelimitedDataFile is similar to *XyDataFile*. Unlike *XyDataFile* format (X-Y-Y…), *DelimitedDataFile* reads in files with a format of (X-Y-X-Y…). Another difference is that a *DelimitedDataFile* can be displayed and edited in the Properties Dialog in the same manner as an XML file.

gov.usgs.sfhydro.data.Db1DataFile is a legacy USGS format. It reads 13 lines of header information, followed by space-delimited column data of the form "_YY_MM_DD_TTTT" where "_" represents spaces and "TTTT" represents the time, in decimal hours, multiplied by 100. All columns to the right of the date and time are considered to be data. The first line of the file is used as the title. The 13th line is used to determine the title of each data series. The fields are separated by underscore characters, with the first four fields reserved for the date and time columns. All other header lines are ignored. Currently, Gr has no output capability for this format.

Here is a sample of data in *Db1DataFile* format:

```
Station ID: 182130 Collection agency = USGS
 Record start: 10/ 8/97 (mon/day/yr), Record end: ??/??/??
 Record length = ?? days
 Station Latitude = 38 3 30 N, Longitude = 122 14 24 W
 Time meridian = 120W Area = Carq. Strait
 Delta discharge average = ??. cfs., (std. dev.) ??.
 Water level time-series mean = ?? ft.
 Gage datum = NGVD 1929 + 10.00 ft.
 Water level (WL) data in feet.
_YR_MO_DA__TIME____WL
 97 10 8 1125 10.50
 97 10 8 1150 10.57
 97 10 8 1175 10.65
 97 10 8 1200 10.76
 97 10 8 1225 10.91
 97 10 8 1250 11.00
```

gov.usgs.sfhydro.data.Db2DataFile is a legacy USGS format for daily output. It reads seven lines of header information, followed by space-delimited column data of the form "YYMMDD", followed by columns of data. The first line of the file is used as the title. The seventh line is used to determine the title of each data series. The fields are separated by underscore characters, with the first field reserved for the date column. All other header lines are ignored. Currently, Gr has no output capability for this format.

Here is a sample of data in *Db2DataFile* format:

```
DAILY DISCHARGES of delta outflow at Sherman Island
NOTE: Discharges measured by 4 ultrasonic velocity meters.
 Positive indicates flow to Bay.
Start date: 10/ 1/97 (mon/day/yr), End date: 12/30/98
Discharges are in cubic feet per second (no data = -999999.)
 YYMMDD____Q=cfs.
 971001 21000.
 971002 12700.
 971003 -999999.
 971004 2880.
```

gov.usgs.sfhydro.data.Dwr1DataFile is a time-series format used for some of the data available on the California Department of Water Resources web site (California Department of Water Resources, accessed March 24, 2008). It reads four lines of header information, followed by space-delimited column data. The first column is the date in the form "DDMMMYYYY_TTTT" where "_" represents a space and "TTTT" represents the time as hour and minutes ("HHMM"). These date and time columns are followed by columns of data. All of the header lines are ignored. Currently, Gr has no output capability for this format.

Here is a sample of data in *Dwr1DataFile* format:

```
/HIST+CHAN/RSAN007/STAGE//15MIN/DWR-CD-SURFWATER/
 20353
TYPE: inst-val
UNITS: feet
30NOV1997 2400 0.07000
01DEC1997 0015 0.35000
01DEC1997 0030 0.62000
01DEC1997 0045 0.88000
01DEC1997 0100 1.13000
```

gov.usgs.sfhydro.data.Noaa1DataFile is a time-series format used for some of the data available on the National Oceanic and Atmospheric Administration (NOAA) web site (National Oceanic and Atmospheric Administration, accessed March 24, 2008). There is no header and all of the columns are separated by commas and optional spaces. The first column is ignored. The second column is the date in the form "YYYY/MM/DD" in double quotes. The third column is the time in the form "HH:MM" in double quotes. The fourth column is the data. All other columns are ignored. Currently, Gr has no output capability for this format.

Here is a sample of data in *Noaa1DataFile* format:

```
"9414750","1997/11/30","16:00", -0.536, 0.009,0,0
"9414750","1997/11/30","17:00", -0.848, 0.005,0,0
"9414750","1997/11/30","18:00", -1.037, 0.003,0,0
"9414750","1997/11/30","19:00", -1.018, 0.004,0,0
"9414750","1997/11/30","20:00", -0.796, 0.002,0,0
"9414750","1997/11/30","21:00", -0.390, 0.007,0,0
"9414750","1997/11/30","22:00", 0.031, 0.005,0,0
```

gov.usgs.gr.data.DelimitedDataFile reads and writes data in a basic column format of decimal numbers delimited by characters, such as spaces or commas.

gov.usgs.gr.data.TimeDataFile is similar to *DelimitedDataFile* and reads and writes data in a basic column format with times in the first column and Y values in the other columns. The times are of the format

```
'yyyy/MM/dd HH:mm'
```

The Y values are specified as decimal numbers delimited by spaces, tabs, or commas. The times are combined with each column to form a *TimeSeries*. Here is a sample of data in *TimeDataFile* format:

```
'2001/03/06 13:45', 0.47, 14.46, 14.51, 0.381
'2001/03/06 14:00', 0.93, 14.27, 14.37, 0.718
'2001/03/06 14:15', 1.39, 14.09, 14.18, 1.193
'2001/03/06 14:30', 1.84, 13.92, 14.0, 1.627
```

Appendix B.   Scripting

Gr's scripting facility provides a way to automate common tasks within the program. Using a text editor, a list of simple commands can be written for Gr to execute in succession. Most of the commands mirror something that could be done using the Gr graphical user interface (GUI). The script files are set up identically to template files and can accept non executable comments if they are preceded by a double forward slash or a forward slash-asterisk. Only one command can be given per line, consisting of a case-insensitive keyword followed by one or more parameters in double quotes. All filename parameters are referenced from the current directory unless a full pathname is given. A full pathname must use forward slashes (/), even on Microsoft Windows systems (Microsoft). Using a full pathname will change the current path to that directory, so the filename parameters that follow can omit the full pathname if the files they reference are in that directory.

To execute a script, click the *Open File...* button or select it from the *File* menu (Ctrl+Shift+O), then choose the file that appears in the dialog. If the script file ends in .grs, for "Gr script," it will be recognized and executed automatically. If it has a different extension, choose *gov.usgs.gr.ScriptFile* as the file type in the *File Options* dialog. If Gr encounters any unrecognized commands in the file, it will show an error dialog box, and stop executing the script. If any of the commands in the scripts cause errors, such as a file not being found, Gr will continue executing. Errors will appear in the console window or in popup dialogs.

When Gr starts, it looks for a file called gr_config.grs in the Gr home directory and executes it if it is present. (The Gr home directory is specified by the *gov.usgs.gr.grhome* variable on the command line or in the Gr batch file.) This file can be used to configure Gr to use a certain file format or to do anything else that can be done in a Gr script.

Each time you open or overlay a file, Gr looks for a gr_config.grs file in the same directory as the file. If it is present, it executes the script before opening the file. That way, Gr can be customized to automatically handle different types of data located in different directories.

Below is an explanation of all the available script commands.

Open "filename"	Opens the specified file. Example: Open "c:/test/data.gs"
Overlay "filename"	Overlays the specified file. Example: Overlay "data2.gs"
SaveDataAs "filename"	Saves data to the specified file using the current file format. Example: SaveDataAs "c:/output/newdata.dat"
SaveAsXml "filename"	Saves data to the specified file using the XML format. Example: saveAsXml "c:/output/grplot.xml"
SaveAsPs "filename"	Saves the page as a PostScript file. Example: SaveAsPs "c:/figures/fig1.ps"
OpenScript "filename"	Opens the specified script file and executes it. Example: OpenScript "c:/test/test.grs"
OpenTemplate "filename"	Opens the specified classic template file and applies it to the page. Example: OpenTemplate "c:/test/test.grt"
OpenXmlTemplate "filename"	Opens the specified XML template file and applies it to the page. Example: OpenXmlTemplate "c:/test/plot.xml"
SetFormat "format"	Sets the data file format for all subsequent Open and Overlay operations. Example: SetFormat "gov.usgs.data.XyDataFile"
SetPageFormat "format"	Sets the page format. Example: SetPageFormat "gov.usgs.sfhydro.gr.formats.SlideFormatter"
SelectGraph "graph number"	Selects the specified graph so it can be moved, hidden, or receive pasted curves. Deselects all other graphs. Example: SelectGraph "2"
SelectCurve "graph number and curve number"	Selects all points on the specified curve so it can be cut, copied, or modified. Leaves previously selected curves selected. It is given with the letter "G" followed by the index of its graph and then the letter "C" followed by the index of the curve within the graph. Example: SelectCurve "G3C2"
SelectAll	Selects all points of any curve that is selected partially. Takes no parameters.
DeselectAll	Deselects every point on the page. Takes no parameters.
Cut	Cuts all selected curves and stores them in the buffer. Takes no parameters.
Copy	Copies all selected curves to the buffer. Takes no parameters.
Paste	Pastes the contents of the buffer to the selected graph. Takes no parameters.

Delete	Deletes all selected points. Takes no parameters.
NewGraph	Creates a new, empty graph at the top of the page. Takes no parameters.
HideGraph	Hides the selected graph. Takes no parameters.
MoveGraph "new position"	Moves the selected graph to a new location on the page. The bottom graph is considered number one. Example: `MoveGraph "1"`
SetGraphProperty "key" "value"	Sets the value of the property with the given key for each selected graph. Example: `SetGraphProperty "title" "Graph 1"`
SetCurveProperty "key" "value"	Sets the value of the property with the given key for each selected curve. Example: `SetCurveProperty "color" "Red"`
Godin	Applies the Godin filter to all selected curves. Takes no parameters.
Modify	This is the most complicated command because it takes a variable number of parameters and values of the form `"Parameter=Value"`. The parameters can be given in any order. It works just like the Modify Dialog box. The *Action* parameter has possible values of *None, Add, Sub, Mul, Div, Set*, and *Avg*, the default being *None*. If the *Action* is *Avg*, the span can be specified with the *AvgSpan* parameter, and the number of samples can be specified with the *AvgSamples* parameter. The *Dim* parameter has possible values of *0*, or *X*, to modify the X dimension, and *1*, or *Y*, to modify the Y dimension. The default is *Y*. The *Input* parameter can specify either a number or a curve, using the same format as the SelectCurve script command. The default is *0.0*. The *Interp* parameter has possible values of *Linear* and *Parab*, the default being *Linear*. The *Output* parameter has possible values of *Original* and *New*, with the default being *Original*. The *Interval* parameter has possible values of *C1, C2*, or *Regular*. If the *Interval* is *Regular*, the interval can be specified with the *RegInterval* parameter, and the offset can be specified with the *RegOffset* parameter. The *Resamp* parameter has possible values of *Interp* or *Avg*. Example: `Modify "Action=sub" "Input=G1C4" "Interp=Parab"`
System "command"	Issues a command to the operating system. Example: `System "c:\\windows\\system32\\cmd /c copy c:\\gr.ps c:\\out.ps"`

Here is a sample script file that converts the first curve on the first graph from degrees Fahrenheit to degrees Celsius and then overlays a file in Xy format and applies a previously saved template.

```
// Script for converting degrees F to C.
DeselectAll
SelectCurve "G1C1"
Modify "Action=sub" "Input=32"
Modify "Action=div" "Input=1.8"
DeselectAll
// Overlay another file and apply a template.
Format "gov.usgs.data.XyDataFile"
Overlay "C:/results/file1.txt"
OpenTemplate "C:/templates/t1.grt"
```

Appendix C.   Tips for Working with Red-Green-Blue (RGB) Colors

Most common color monitors use Red-Green-Blue (RGB) color to create the color displayed on the screen. Gr makes use of colors to distinguish its various elements, so it is helpful to have a basic understanding of how the RGB color system works.

RGB is an additive system, as opposed to the Cyan-Magenta-Yellow-Black (CMYK) system, which is a subtractive system used for printed output and is used to produce colors using light. Red, green, and blue are the three color components that are added together. Color monitors vary the amount of red, green, and blue light coming from each pixel to create millions of distinct colors. Each of these spots is tiny and blends with the other spots, resulting in an additive color.

The subtractive system in which "yellow and blue make green" works with paint or ink but not with light. With the RGB system, yellow is not a primary color but a combination of red and green. The following definitions are of some common colors and how they are created with RGB: 0 means a color is fully turned off and 1 means a color is fully turned on.

Note that the cyan is similar to aqua or turquoise, the color magenta is similar to maroon, and brown is the same as dark yellow.

Black is the absence of all light, and white is the presence of all light. A brighter shade of any color is created by multiplying all of the components by some number greater than 1. A darker shade of any color is created by multiplying all the components by some number between 0 and 1.

Gray results whenever all three components are at equal levels and no one color stands out. If a color is dull, but not dark, all three colors probably are at medium levels. The brightest shade of gray is white and the darkest shade is black.

Overall intensity is the sum of all three color components. Human eyes are slightly more sensitive to green than to red and blue, so the green component counts a little more than red and blue. The human eye, in turn, is slightly more sensitive to red than to blue. The differences are on the order of about 10 percent. This can be tested by using Gr's Detailed Status Bar and setting all three color sliders to 0, then increasing each color individually until the color change is perceived.

To create a given color, it should be compared relatively to two of the more basic colors shown in table C1. The levels of each color component will be between their respective levels in the basic colors. For example, to make light yellow, the RGB levels will be somewhere between those of yellow (1, 1, 0) and white (1, 1, 1). That is, red and green would be at the full level, and blue would vary, depending on the level desired of the yellow component.

Choosing a color for a graphical curve should involve considering the adjacent colors for visual contrast and compatibility. For example, bright green contrasts highly against a dark blue background but not against a white background. Objects are seen more easily if their color and overall intensity contrast with the background color.

Inverting the levels of each RGB component often results in an opposing color, such as yellow (1, 1, 0) on blue (0, 0, 1). However, this does not always provide the highest possible contrast. Inverting the intensity also can yield high contrast, such as white on black. White and black, however, are special cases, and other colors never have such highly contrasting opposites. What appears as the highest contrast to your eye for most colors may be a combination of opposing colors and opposing intensities, such as bright yellow (1, 1, 0.3) on dark blue (0, 0, 0.2).

On a black and white device, such as a certain laser printers, contrast can be varied only by varying the overall intensity. A medium red line and a medium blue line will not be distinguishable after being converted to shades of gray.

A final note on color is to remember that red-green color blindness is not uncommon, especially in men. To ensure that everyone can distinguish the color between two curves, ensure that the colors differ in overall intensity or have different levels of blue components.

Table C1.   Examples of basic Red-Green-Blue (RGB) color system combinations.

Color	Red	Green	Blue	Result
Black	0	0	0	
White	1	1	1	
Red	1	0	0	
Green	0	1	0	
Blue	0	0	1	
Yellow	1	1	0	
Magenta	1	0	1	
Cyan	0	1	1	

Table C2.   Examples of ranges of Red-Green-Blue (RGB) color system values.

Color Description	Component Range	Example RGB	Result
Grays	R = G = B		
Skin tones, oranges, gold, browns	R > G > B		
Pinks	R > B > G		
Swamp Green, Chartreuse	G > R > B		
Mint Greens	G > B > R		
Violets, Lavenders	B > R > G		
Electric Blue, Powder Blue	B > G > R		
Dark Colors	(R + G + B) < 1		
Light Colors	(R + G + B) > 2		

Appendix D.   Symbol Indexes

The symbol type for a curve in Gr is an integer index between 0 and 13, as described in the table.

Table D1.   The available symbols, associated indexes, and appearance on PostScript output.

Symbol Index	Symbol Description	Appearance on PostScript Output
0	Single pixel	.
1	Plus sign	+
2	X	×
3	Tick mark	|
4	Hollow circle	○
5	Hollow square	□
6	Hollow upward-pointing triangle	△
7	Hollow downward-pointing triangle	▽
8	Hollow diamond	◇
9	Filled circle	●
10	Filled square	■
11	Filled upward-pointing triangle	▲
12	Filled downward-pointing triangle	▼
13	Filled diamond	◆

Appendix E.   Contact Information

```
John M. Donovan
jmd@usgs.gov
(916)278-3120
Placer Hall
6000 J Street
Sacramento, CA 95819-6129
```

Manuscript approved for publication, August 27, 2009
Prepared by the USGS Enterprise Publishing Network,
Publishing Service Center, Sacramento, California

For more information concerning the research in this report, contact the
  California Water Science Center Director,
  U.S. Geological Survey, 6000 J Street
  Sacramento, California 95819
  http://ca.water.usgs.gov